PARABLES
OF THE
KINGDOM
MORRIS L. VENDEN

Pacific Press Publishing Association
Boise, Idaho 4438
Montemorelos, Nuevo Leon, Mexico
Oshawa, Ontario, Canada

Edited by Don Mansell
Designed by Tim Larson
Cover Illustration by Lars Justinen
Type set in 10/12 Century Schoolbook

Pacific Press Publishing Association
Boise, Idaho
Montemorelos, Nuevo Leon, Mexico
Oshawa, Ontario, Canada

Library of Congress Cataloging in Publication Data

Venden, Morris L.
  Parables of the kingdom.

  1. Jesus Christ—Parables. I. Title.
BT375.2.V46   1986   226'.806   86-22641

ISBN 0-8163-0680-X

86 87 88 89 90 • 5 4 3 2 1

Contents

"Seek ye first the kingdom of God, and his righteousness; and all these things shall be added unto you." Matthew 6:33.

Introduction

Everybody enjoys stories! Adults try to pretend that stories are for children, but have you ever watched their faces when a "children's story" is being told? They are often more intent on hearing what happens next than are the children!

There have been a lot of good storytellers. You may have even had the privilege of hearing stories from one of the *great* storytellers, who is able to make you see and feel and hear what's happening in the stories he tells—and remember them ever after. But the greatest storyteller of all time was Jesus Himself. Frequently He caught the attention of the people by the simple means of telling a story.

Jesus' stories often were in the form of parables. Parables are stories with a double application—yet the fact is that most stories are parables. Students of literature are educated to look for the story behind the story. Psychologists and counselors are trained to listen to the stories people tell, to find evidence of deeper communication than the stories themselves.

In parables and stories and comparisons, Jesus found the best method for communicating divine truth. One of His purposes in teaching through parables was to reveal that truth. By connecting spiritual lessons with scenes familiar to His hearers, He was able to help them understand and remember His teachings. Another purpose Jesus had in using parables was the exact opposite—His parables concealed truth. Thus He was able to speak out against sin and error in such a way that His enemies could find nothing in His words to use against Him. Often, in spite of themselves, they would be caught up in the stories He was telling and condemn themselves.

Many of the stories Jesus told began with the words, "The kingdom of heaven is like unto." He must have known how hard it is for us who live under the kingdoms of this earth to understand the nature of the kingdom of heaven.

Stories abound that tell us what the earthly kingdoms are like. Even in the days of Christ there must have been plenty of stories told about the kings and queens who exercised arbitrary power, who were greedy, self-seeking, and powerfully rich. Over the centuries there have been unnumbered stories of wars and conquests and battles. There have been stories of the struggles and hardships of the common people in society, as they try to live under the rule of the kingdom that ruled over them. There have been stories of insurrection and rebellion which were met by harshness and cruelty as the rulers tried to maintain the force of their control over a dissatisfied people.

But in the parables of Jesus we are given a glimpse into the kingdom of heaven, which operates on a completely different set of values than the kingdoms of this earth. We hear Him describe the basis of the kingdom of heaven to come—and also the kingdom of grace in the heart, which is the beginning of the heavenly kingdom.

If we are not comfortable with the kingdom of heaven now, we will not feel at ease with that kingdom throughout eternity. The kingdom of heaven is on the gift system—the kingdoms of earth are based on merit and on earning your own rewards. The kingdom of heaven offers service for others as the highest privilege—the earthly kingdoms seek service *from* others as evidence of highest honor. The heavenly kingdom works through the freedom of love—the kingdoms of earth use force to accomplish their goals.

Does the prospect of living forever in the heavenly country sound good to you? Are you attracted by the prospect of fellowship with Jesus here and now? One of the simplest methods for understanding what the kingdom of heaven is all about is to be found in a study of Jesus' *Parables of the Kingdom.*

Chapter 1
The Sower, the Seed, and the Soil

Have you ever planted a garden? Probably most of us can re member working in the soil, with a little help from Mom or Dad, and planting those radish seeds. Why was it always rad- ishes? Then we would go to bed and rush out the first thing in the morning to see how the radishes were coming, right? Re- member what came up first? It wasn't radishes—it was the weeds!

But as soon as the first little radish sprouts appeared, I know what I did. And perhaps I wasn't the only person ever to do such a thing. I pulled them up to see if there were any radishes. I can remember pulling one a day to see how they were coming along—and that didn't help things a bit.

If they didn't come up after a few days, I would go and dig for them, to see where they were. I've even done that with grass seed!

But there's a lot to be learned out there in the garden, and Jesus Himself used parables about the garden on more than one occasion. In fact, it seemed to be one of His favorite themes for presenting truth about the kingdom of heaven.

Let's notice one of His major parables, found in Luke 8. "And when much people were gathered together, and were come to him out of every city, he spake by a parable: a sower went out to sow his seed: and as he sowed, some fell by the way side; and it was trodden down, and the fowls of the air devoured it. And some fell upon a rock; and as soon as it was sprung up, it with- ered away, because it lacked moisture. And some fell among thorns; and the thorns sprang up with it, and choked it. And other fell on good ground, and sprang up, and bare fruit an hundredfold. And when he had said these things, he cried, He that hath ears to hear, let him hear. And his disciples asked him, saying, What might this parable be?" Verses 4-9.

Well, when Jesus stands up and cries for those of us who have ears to hear, then the message must be rather important. Jesus said something like this on several occasions. He told the people, "Go and learn what this means," when He said, "I came not to call the righteous, but sinners to repentance." So let's try to hear what He was saying in this parable about the sower, the seed, and the soil.

The Sower

Who does the sower represent? The Sower is Jesus—He was referring to Himself. He came from the city that has jasper walls and twelve foundations to an unfriendly country.

In the days of Christ, farmers didn't live out on the farm. They were village farmers. It wasn't safe to stay out in the country. The cities had walls for protection. You can go to parts of the world today where the remains of those days still stand. There were walls to keep people safe from robbers and thieves and murderers. The unfortunate man who was beaten up by the thieves on the Jericho Road and was helped by the good Samaritan was a sample of what things were like in the days of Jesus. Farmers lived in the city behind safe walls and went out into the countryside in the daytime to sow their seed.

Jesus left a friendly city, a heavenly city, where He was adored by angels, and all the created universe worshiped before Him. He came to an unfriendly country, outside the walls of safety, to a place of thieves and robbers and murderers. He took all the risks necessary in order to plant the seed. This is the kind of person the sower was.

Do you like to think of Jesus as a farmer? It's not Farmer Brown or Farmer Jones; it's Farmer Jesus. How does that sound? It's not irreverent to call Him Farmer Jesus, for in His life here in this earth, He put His stamp of approval on hard physical work. He's the One who worked for eighteen years in the carpenter shop in Nazareth, planing wood and sawing boards.

I'm glad that Jesus didn't live in a palace, aren't you? I'm glad that Jesus was a poor person who knew the meaning of hard work. By being this kind of person He could reach everybody. And so He came forth to sow.

The Seed

What is the seed? Jesus explains the parable, and so you know, if you've read the rest of Luke 8, that the seed is the Word of God. Nothing more, nothing less. The Word of God has power to produce life and growth and fruit in the soul.

It is still true today. We can have everything else besides the Word of God. Sometimes we try to meet people with philosophy and psychology and entertainment and all kinds of things. Sometimes we think our boys and girls need entertainment or gimmicks to keep their attention. Maybe we need to remember the power that is in the Word of God, that "liveth and abideth forever." When we join Jesus in sowing the seed of the gospel, it is the Word of God that is the seed. That's where it's at.

The Soil

But what about the soil? There were four kinds of soil mentioned. It almost sounds like predestination, doesn't it? Were you born as hard-packed wayside or rocky soil or thorny soil? Or were you born with good soil? Do you think you can identify which kind of soil is in your own heart? What if you discover that the soil in your heart is no good? Is there anything you can do about it? Keep these questions in mind as we think about the four kinds of soil Jesus talked about in this parable.

The Wayside

The wayside is ground that is packed down and hard from being tramped over. If it isn't actually the path, it's at least right next to it. It's the ground alongside the road that is almost as hard as the road itself. It's where the brown paper bags lie and the broken bottles and the M & M wrappers. It is filled with debris. It's not an attractive place, and certainly not a good place to sow seed.

It could represent the kind of person who has a hard-beaten path from his house to the church, but who has allowed the debris of cherished sin and habit and neglect to fill up his life. The wayside ground is not subject to change—in fact, it is resistent to change. The wayside hearers believe that whatever was good enough for father or mother is good enough for them. Their religion is conventional and consists of going through the forms. If there's a crack in the clutter where the seed can fall and spring up, then the predatory birds come along and get it—and there are plenty of predatory birds in the kingdom of this world.

So the seed that falls onto the wayside ground doesn't stand much of a chance. If we are able to squeeze Jesus into the cracks, that's about all He can expect. There is no hope for a harvest or for fruit to His glory. It doesn't look too good for the heart with the wayside soil.

Rocky Soil

Let's consider the second type of soil, the rocky soil. You'd think that the seed that falls there doesn't have much of a chance either. But even among rocks there usually is a bit of dust, and it's amazing what can spring up after a rain—tiny green shoots on what looks like bare rock. These might last for a half a day, or maybe for a day and a half. But they don't last long because there isn't enough soil for them to take root. The sun scorches them, or the next rain washes them away, and they are soon gone.

Rocky soil could represent the kind of religious experience that is here today and gone tomorrow, the kind of person who can go through a revival and an apostasy all the same week. This could represent the emotional religion, dependent upon the right singing, the right nostalgia, the right tear-jerking stories. But soon after the emotional high is over, things are right back where they started.

This soil represents the person who responds only with his emotions, and such an experience is neither deep nor lasting— it is just the impulse of the moment, just the reaction for the day. It is a sort of rock-and-roll religion that works the nervous system, but doesn't change the heart. There may be a seeming conversion under the thrill of the moment. But as soon as the stimulus is removed, the spiritual life dies out—sometimes overnight. It doesn't look too good for the heart with the rocky soil.

Thorny Ground

Some seed fell among thorny ground. We find thorns and weeds are everywhere, don't we? They don't require culti- ivation. They can spring up spontaneously. When our family lived in Nebraska a few years ago, we had a seven-acre piece of ground that was covered with those purple thistles. The weeds seemed to multiply a thousand times over every spring and summer—and they didn't require any work, either. If we had wanted to raise purple thistles, all we would have had to do would have been to lie in the hammock and let it happen!

Well, some seed fell among the thorns, and even though the soil underneath might have been all right, there were too many thorns. Many of us, perhaps, identify with this soil. One might argue as to whether or not he was wayside or rocky soil, but there's no mistaking thorny ground. It's easy to see the thorns in our lives, the things that choke out the good seed. They can easily be seen everywhere.

What are some of the thorns in our lives? Some of them could be the pleasures of the world, maybe even innocent pleasures— like playing tennis, for instance! Something that is good in it-self becomes a thorn when it crowds out the good seed. Another kind of thorns would be life's cares, perplexities, and sorrows. There are plenty of those to demand our attention, no matter who we are. The problem of keeping body and soul together can take a lot of time and energy. The poor fear for want, and the rich for loss. Both can become preoccupied with the cares of this life.

Thorns can take the form of sorrow and heartache. Sorrow and grief are the common lot of humanity, but some of us allow the devil to turn these things into thorns—thorns that prevent us from seeing Jesus anymore.

Then there are the faults of others. How many times have people stumbled over the faults of those around them? We've all experienced it to some degree. The faults of others can turn into thorns in our pathway if we allow them to keep our attention from Jesus and the things of heaven. And our own faults and imperfections can accomplish the same thing.

What can one do about thorns—the weeds and the thistles that prevent the growth of the gospel seed? There are a lot of thorns out there—and it doesn't look too good for the thorny soil.

The Good Soil

What is the good soil? It is those who receive the seed with an honest and good heart. That sounds appealing, doesn't it? Do you have an honest heart, a good heart? How many hearts of that kind are there?

It's common to hear Christians pray for the "honest in heart." But, have you ever heard someone pray for the Lord's blessing on the dishonest in heart? I hadn't, until one day I heard someone say, "Lord, bless all the dishonest in heart!" Surely the dishonest in heart need some prayers too.

One time at a campmeeting I heard the speaker get up and ask, "How many of you have been praying for Khrushchev?" Not a soul raised his hand! Then he said, "I've been praying for Khrushchev lately. He seems to be standing in the need of prayer. I think he'd make a wonderful preacher, don't you?"

What about the apostle Paul? Before his experience on the Damascus Road, he certainly did not appear to be a good candidate for leadership in the early church. He is frequently depicted holding the coats of the men who were stoning Stephen. But that was just the beginning. From doing that he went on to become directly responsible for the death and imprisonment of many of the Christian believers. He tells us so.

But God could see into the heart, and He saw good soil there. And one day He stepped in and stopped Saul in his tracks, and Saul became Paul, the mighty preacher and evangelist and author and missionary.

So how can we judge what is in someone's heart? We don't know the roots, the background of those around us. Only God knows what makes an honest heart. Only He knows where the good soil is to be found—and some of the places where good soil can be discovered turn out to be a surprise to many of us.

What is good soil? Here are a few clues. It is soil that yields to the conviction of the Holy Spirit, admits its need, maintains a continual, personal receiving of life from the heavenly Gardener. And it is in this kind of soil that the perfect fruit of faith and meekness and love matures.

How can you be good soil? Or can you? Is a person simply predestined to be good soil? or wayside soil? or rocky soil? or thorny soil? But if one isn't predestined to be a particular kind of soil, how does one become good soil? Does it sound attractive to you?

Jesus never taught predestination. The Bible doesn't teach it. This parable is saying that in every heart are all four kinds of soil.

Every Kind of Soil

Haven't you noticed samples of each kind of soil in your own heart? We all know what it's like to be wayside soil on some things, if not on all things. If someone gets up and talks against one kind of sin of which I disapprove, I'm good soil. My folks, for instance, raised me with certain inhibitions. Some things do not appeal to me simply because of my tastes and inclinations and personality. So when I hear those things condemned, I'm good soil.

But if someone gets up and talks against one of my besetting sins, all of a sudden I'm wayside soil.

It is possible to be wayside soil or rocky soil or thorny soil on one thing, and good soil on something else. We have all experienced it and find that even when it comes to the gospel itself and relating to the call of Jesus to the human heart, that we give mixed responses.

But there is good soil in every heart. And the great Farmer, the Sower of the seed, Jesus Himself, is anxious to reach that good soil with the seed of the gospel. He will try every means possible to reach the good soil in your heart and sow the seed of His Word, that it may produce a harvest to His glory.

I wish I didn't have thorny soil. I don't like the hardness I sometimes feel in my heart. Sometimes I find it hard to change some of my ideas. But is there something I can do about it? What can I do to help the Gardener rid my life of thorns and stones and hard-packed earth?

It's intriguing to consider just exactly what it is that we can do in this process of seed-sowing and growth in our lives. Have you ever tried to get the weeds out of your soul soil? Have you? How can it be done? Here's a parable that may help you think this through.

What Can the Soil Do?

This is the story of a plot of ground that wanted to be a garden. The story actually begins with the Farmer, who purchased the plot of ground at great expense. He then provided some seed of excellent quality and came to the plot of ground and sowed the seed.

Well, the plot of ground rejoiced. It had always wanted to be a garden. And it began immediately to try to do its part toward becoming a garden of beauty and fruitfulness. It began to look at itself and discovered to its dismay that it was covered with a number of unsightly weeds. There were thorns and thistles and briers and brambles, and the plot of ground was concerned and ashamed. Before the coming of the Farmer it hadn't paid much attention to such things, and the weeds had made terrible inroads. Their roots were deeply entrenched in the soil.

"How can I receive any benefit from the seed while all these weeds are growing unchecked?" wondered the plot of ground. "Everybody knows that a garden must be weeded in order for the seed to grow."

So it began immediate efforts to try to remove the weeds. It wanted to cooperate with the Farmer so that the time would come as quickly as possible when it would no longer be just an ugly weed patch, but would become a lovely garden.

The plot of ground struggled and fretted. It sincerely wanted to get rid of its weeds, but the problem was figuring out how. All the instruction about weed-pulling seemed to be vague and contradictory. The plot of ground heard from one source that if it would get rid of the leaves and stems, the Farmer would then be willing to pull out the roots. But it discovered it was too weak to get rid of the leaves and stems.

It was told that if a plot of ground did its part, then the Farmer would do His part. But the plot of ground seemed unable to do any part of the weed-pulling for itself. It was often told to try hard to overcome the weeds, but it didn't exactly know how to do that either, and when the weeds were still apparent, week after week, those around the plot of ground, and even the plot of ground itself began to wonder if it were really sincere in wanting to get rid of the weeds.

Someone suggested to the plot of ground that if it would not try to remove the weeds from the whole garden all at once, but would concentrate on removing just one weed at a time, that would be easier. But the plot of ground found itself unable to remove even one weed.

At times the plot of ground almost gave up in discouragement at the lack of progress made, but then it would once again picture the garden it longed to become, and it would again put forth earnest efforts to try to get rid of the weeds. But all of the efforts of the plot of ground to rid itself of the thorns and briers ended in nothing.

One day the plot of ground was forced to admit that it would never become a beautiful garden on its own, and that day the Farmer came to the plot of ground with some terrific news. The Farmer had come often before, but the plot of ground had been so busy struggling with the weeds that it hadn't really taken time to listen. The Farmer told the plot of ground something that was almost impossible to believe. It seemed at first glance to go contrary to everything the plot of ground had ever heard about gardening. Here is what the Farmer said: "It is not the responsibility of the garden to get rid of the weeds. That is the work of the Gardener."

It Is the Gardener Who Pulls the Weeds

Well, you can see right away why the plot of ground had a hard time with the response. No wonder the plot of ground had trouble with the Farmer's announcement.

But unless the plot of ground accepted the Farmers offer, it must give up all hope of becoming a beautiful garden So the plot of ground surrendered to the Farmer and allowed Him to pull the weeds. And the first thing you know, the weeds were being pulled up—by the roots, not just the leaves and stems went. The whole plant was uprooted and taken far away from the plot of ground. Then in their place good seeds were sown, and the garden began to grow and develop.

As time passed, the plot of ground, which was now a beautiful garden, continued to allow the Farmer to do His work. And the garden continued to do its work. It continued to accept the seed that the Farmer sowed, drank deeply of the water the Farmer showered, and basked in the sunshine that the Farmer provided. The plants in the garden grew and grew and brought forth fruit—some an hundredfold, some sixty, and some thirty.

Chapter 2
The Tares

There is coming a day when everyone who has ever lived or died will meet for the first and last time. And when that day comes, everyone from the least to the greatest—and even the devil himself—will bow in acknowledgement of the truth that God has been fair and just in His dealings in the great controversy. He has never overstepped Himself. He has always given His creatures the benefit of the doubt. He has never taken advantage, even of His enemies.

The kingdoms of this world don't operate on those kinds of values. In the worldly kingdom, any chance you have to get what you want, you take it. Literature has glorified the chivalry of the medieval knights, but we see little of it in the world today. Human beings are not known for allowing their opponents to have the advantage, if they can prevent it. But the kingdom of heaven operates on an entirely different principle.

Jesus talked about this principle in His parable about the tares and the wheat, found in Matthew 13. "Another parable put he forth unto them saying, The kingdom of heaven is likened unto a man which sowed good seed in his field: but while men slept, his enemy came and sowed tares among the wheat, and went his way. But when the blade was sprung up, and brought forth fruit, then appeared the tares also. So the servants of the householder came and said unto him, Sir, didst thou sow good seed in thy field? from whence then hath it tares? He said unto them, An enemy hath done this. The servants said

17

unto him, Wilt thou then that we go and gather them up? But he said, Nay; lest while ye gather up the tares, ye root up also the wheat with them. Let both grow together until the harvest: and in the time of harvest I will say to the reapers, Gather ye together first the tares, and bind them in bundles to burn them: but gather the wheat into my barn." Matthew 13:24-30.

Jesus explained the meaning of this parable to His disciples in verses 36-43 of the same chapter. The separation between the righteous and the wicked is to take place at the end of the world. And until that time, both will be allowed to grow together.

In every parable of Jesus, spiritual truth was given that went deeper than just the surface. He designed His parables to be pondered and treasured, so that there would be ever new unfoldings of truth to the one who sought to understand their meaning. A parable is like an onion! How's that for making a parable about parables? There are layers of understanding, all fitted together, but each one unique. Will you join me in "peeling the onion" in this parable of the tares?

The Field Is the World

Jesus told His disciples where to begin their search. Apparently they didn't understand anything about what He was trying to say, for He gave several parables, one right after the other, as recorded in Matthew 13. And the disciples asked for no explanation of the last few parables in the sequence except for the one about the tares.

Jesus opened up the first "layer of the onion" to get His disciples started thinking. He was the Master Teacher and knew that students are better able to remember what they have searched out and thought out for themselves than what they are simply told.

When I was in college, my major professor used to use this technique on his students. There were many times when we'd leave his class to head for the library for further study, instead of going to the gym or the student center to relax. I remember one day a fiery young man in the front row stood up and said,

"OK, professor, you've frustrated us long enough. Now give us the answer." It didn't work. He still made us puzzle it out for ourselves.

Such was the method Jesus used with the people of His day. He gave them enough on which to get started, and no more. So He said, The field is the world. In the world, there are righteous and wicked. Both will grow together until the harvest—the end of the world.

When you look at the field as the world, is there any question in your mind as to the truth but that an enemy has been at work? How truthfully we can echo the words "an enemy hath done this" when we see the pain and sorrow and sickness and death and heartache in a world gone wrong. God is not the one responsible for the sin in the world. The enemy is the one to blame.

Yet God allows this situation to continue. He is directly responsible for keeping the heart beating in the chest of the one who curses Him. He sends the rain on the just and the unjust. God does not execute final judgment until the judgment day. He lets both grow together until the harvest, when the character of each is fully manifested before all the watching universe. God even keeps the devil himself supplied with life. No wonder, in the end, every knee bows, and every tongue confesses to God's fairness and love; for it is only when the harvest is fully come that God will give the command for the tares in His world field to be destroyed.

The Field Is the Church

Let's look at the parable a little more closely now and examine the field of the church. Does the parable apply there as well? Are there righteous and wicked enrolled in the church, or are the wicked only "out there"? You know the answer to that one, don't you?

Within the church, the tares and the wheat can resemble each other very closely. God didn't design that there should be false brethren within His church. Again we can say, "an enemy hath done this." The devil is active in evangelism! He works to convert people to the church, while keeping them from becoming converted to Christ. The tares in the church give the enemy a tremendous advantage. They may retard the growth of the wheat. They may keep things astir, so that the truth is misrepresented. Church members who speak words that stir up strife are doing Satan's work much more effectively than those who are openly his own subjects.

It is a well-known fact that in times of war, a spy can accomplish far more toward overcoming the stronghold of the enemy than can a soldier. Nations at war expect and are prepared for attacks from without. But they are not always prepared for attack from within and for this reason it is a most effective tool. Over and over the devil has used this tool to attempt to destroy God's church.

We are warned by this parable against the work of trying to identify and separate the wheat from the tares in the church. Both may look alike for a time. If we trust our own understanding, we are liable to make many mistakes.

Look at the church to whom Jesus gave this parable in the first place. It had twelve members. Outwardly, there were problems. There was bickering and arguing about who was to be the greatest. There were tempers and poor judgment and proud hearts. In fact, probably the one who looked like he had the fewest problems was Judas. It's easy for us today to see where Judas went wrong, because the "harvest" has already come for Judas. But for the disciples back then, he looked for sure like fine wheat. And some of the rest of them were a mess!

But notice again what this parable teaches about how Jesus works with tares. He doesn't come in with His sharp sickle and start cutting. He waits. He watches. And He asks us to wait and watch until the natural outcome is manifest.

Christ knew, when He permitted Judas to connect with Him as one of the Twelve, that Judas was possessed of the demon of selfishness. He knew that this professed disciple would betray Him, and yet He did not separate him from the other disciples and send him away. He was preparing the minds of these men for His death and ascension, and He foresaw that should He dismiss Judas, Satan would use him to spread reports that would be difficult to meet and explain. The leaders of the Jewish nation were watching and searching for something that they could use to make of no effect the words of Christ. The Saviour knew that Judas, if dismissed, could so misconstrue and mystify His statements that the Jews would accept a false version of His words, using this version to bring terrible harm to the disciples and to leave on the minds of Christ's enemies the impression that the Jews were justified in taking the attitude that they did toward Jesus and His disciples.

Christ did not, therefore, banish Judas from His presence, but kept him by His side, where He could counteract his influence against His work.

Jesus not only accepts those whom the devil brings into His church to harm it, but He does everything He can do to win those very ones to Himself! That's how the kingdom of God operates.

The story is told of someone questioning Abraham Lincoln on his practice of making peace with his enemies, even giving them positions of trust in his cabinet. "Why," he was asked, "don't you destroy your enemies?"

He replied, "Have I not destroyed my enemies when I make them my friends?"

Jesus almost won Judas! And only eternity will reveal how many of the "spies" the enemy has brought into the church have been reached with the gospel, because of their close association with the spiritual things!

The Field Is Your Heart

Are you willing to try for one more layer of understanding? There are some who will have a hard time listening to this next application of the parable of the tares. But ponder it, and see if you recognize truth.

In the field of your heart, there may be tares along with the wheat. Have you ever been aware of them? Have you ever decided that it was your work to uproot them? This parable of the tares teaches that the work of uprooting tares is to be God's work, directed by Him.

We would surely agree that when we become aware of the tares in our own hearts (even after the gospel seed has found lodgment there), that it is the work of an enemy. God is not responsible for the tares. But is it possible that God sometimes deals with the tares in our hearts in the same way He deals with tares in the church and in the world? Could it be possible that even on this level, He allows a process of time and growth and development, in order that the nature of the plants may be fully recognized.

We would not go so far as some who think that the harvest at the end of the world takes care of all of the imperfections in our characters. No, the harvest represents the maturing of the fruits of the Spirit in the life, the development of the character. However, doesn't it sometimes take time before we can distinguish between that which is fault and that which is virtue? So, even in the field of the heart, had we not better leave the work of weeding with the Gardener?

As we consider this possibility, let us look at the experience of Peter. Peter had accepted Jesus and followed Him. He spent time with Him day by day. Fellowship with Christ was his highest joy. Peter had been converted. At this point someone is sure to remember the words of Jesus when He said, "When you are converted. . . ." But since conversion is a daily matter, it was a reconversion referred to in that passage, not the initial experience of conversion.

Peter had been sent forth with the twelve, and again with the seventy. He had healed the sick and cleansed the lepers and cast out demons and raised the dead. Jesus had told him his name was in the book of life. See Luke 10:20. And we know that unless the new birth has taken place, no one can even see the kingdom of heaven. See John 3. So the evidence is that Peter had been converted.

But Peter had a problem. He had several problems, in fact, but the basis of them all was that he was self-sufficient. He didn't realized his own condition. He knew he sinned on occasion. He was with the disciples who lagged behind Jesus on the road to Capernaum so they could bicker and argue more comfortably. But Peter thought he could handle things himself.

The night on the lake, when he almost drowned, should have alerted him to his danger, but he didn't heed the warning. There were tares in Peter's heart, but he thought he could handle them himself. And the worst tares of all, he didn't even recognize.

Peter was so sure of himself that he told Jesus that even if the rest of the disciples forsook Him, he would not. His self-assurance was the worst of his problems, and he didn't even identify it as being a problem.

What did Jesus do? He dealt with Peter as He deals with the tares in the church. He allowed time for his harvest to grow. He gave him time to see for himself the difference between the tares and the wheat, so that when the tares were uprooted, Peter would not misunderstand and think Christ was making a mistake.

One time I was talking to another pastor about a particular church member, who was a "good liver"! This person wouldn't think of doing anything wrong. But he was not interested in spiritual things. He was satisfied with going through the form and keeping God at arm's length, while he lived out his spotless life apart from Christ.

And the other pastor said, "I think before that person can be truly converted, he will have to commit some terrible sin."

What a thing to say! Haven't we been promised not to be tempted above what we're able to bear? Surely God wouldn't permit someone to sin in order to save him. That doesn't make sense!

Then I remembered Peter! Peter was a better man after his fall. He learned a lesson that apparently he could learn only through failure. And the Lord permitted him to fall, all the while promising him forgiveness when he turned again and repented of his sin.

Those who recognize their weakness are more likely to trust in a Power higher then themselves. And while they look to God, Satan has no power over them. But those who trust in themselves are easily defeated. The self-sufficient one, who like Peter, acts as if he knew more than his Lord, is allowed to go on in his supposed strength. And sometimes the shock of failure leads to the realization of the weakness of self which could not be realized in any other way.

We long for victory and power in the Christian life, and we often see failures that let us know we are not yet perfect. But God works patiently from cause to effect. The tares that we see may be the result of a deeper problem. And so God takes the time to allow things to develop, in order for us to understand our need. In the end, He brings us to the point of recognizing the tares for what they really are and of allowing Him to remove them from our lives. But there is a process involved, even in the field of the heart.

Our part is to continue to seek Him, to behold Him, to fellowship with Him, so that the process of growth can be completed in our lives. Then we can join Peter in realizing our helplessness and our total dependence upon Him. So long as we continue to seek His control of our lives, He will not leave us, even when He permits us to fall. His goal for us is to bring us to the *inside* of the celestial city, to kneel with the ransomed from all ages, and join with them in proclaiming, "Great and marvellous are thy works, Lord God Almighty; just and true are thy ways, thou King of saints. Who shall not fear thee, O lord, and glorify thy name? for thou only art holy: for all nations shall come and worship before thee; for thy judgments are made manifest." Revelation 15:3, 4.

Chapter 3
Jesus, the Good Samaritan

I am a gambler! Oh, I don't mean the kind that spends Sundays at the local gambling hall. But I find it challenging to try to make it in my car to the next town on empty! My family does not particularly appreciate my gambling instinct, so when they are with me, they have a way of controlling this propensity. But believe it or not, through this "vegetarian" form of gambling I have met many nice people. Perhaps it could even be considered a form of witnessing!

One day I was cooling my heels by the side of the highway in California, on an off ramp. The people in the Lincoln Continentals went by and so did the people wearing the business suits. People with the fancy vans went past, and the Winnebagos as well. Then along came a young man with long hair and a beard, driving a battered pickup. He stopped, and not only took me to get gas, but brought me back and made sure my car was going before he went on his way. I've thought a lot about that experience since that time.

The Good Samaritan sometimes is a surprising type of person, isn't he? It's an old, old story, but let's look at it, and maybe we can find something new. Jesus gave a mini-parable in Matthew 13:52, about things old and new. "Then said he unto them, Therefore every scribe which is instructed unto the kingdom of heaven is like unto a man that is an householder, which bringeth forth out of his treasure things new and old."

That's one of the exciting things about the kingdom of heaven. It's not possible to exhaust the supply of treasure. We understand that even throughout eternity we will be studying things old and new. And sometimes it is the new twist that brings a breakthrough to someone when he sees truth he hasn't noticed before. Every new disclosure of the Saviour's love turns the balance for some soul in one direction or the other.

So let's look for the old and new in this story of the Good Samaritan, recorded in Luke 10.

The Jewish leaders were out to get Jesus, so they engaged one of their champions, a sharp lawyer, to try to trip Him up. They felt this lawyer was capable of tangling with Jesus. They had hopes that with his fine, argumentative mind, he could get Jesus out on thin ice and then sink Him. The one thing they failed to allow for was that this lawyer they sent to trap Jesus was a sincere seeker for truth himself. And he had been watching Jesus. He was glad for an excuse to initiate personal contact for his own sake.

Beginning with verse 25 of Luke 10, "And, behold, a certain lawyer stood up, and tempted him, saying, Master, what shall I do to inherit eternal life?" This was typical of the religion of his day, and it's still typical today. Human nature hasn't changed. Even in the Christian faith, we find that most Christians think of the Christian life in terms of doing, rather than in terms of knowing. One of the truths that Jesus came to present was that the Christian life and eternal life are not based upon what you do, they are based upon Who you know. He is the One who said it in John 17:3, "This is life eternal, that they might know thee the only true God, and Jesus Christ, whom thou hast sent." So the Christian life is not based upon behavior, but on relationship. You might expect Jesus to go straight into a discourse on that, but instead, Jesus went on to say, "What is written in the law? How readest thou?" Sounds like a legalistic answer, doesn't it?

The lawyer responded in kind. "He answering said, Thou shalt love the Lord thy God with all thy heart, and with all thy soul, and with all thy strength, and with all thy mind; and thy neighbour as thyself. And he said unto him, Thou hast answered right: this do, and thou shalt live."

As you know, if you have studied Jesus' method of teaching,

He was not in the habit of giving pat answers. He knew, as the Master Teacher, that the way to teach is to lead the student into an atmosphere where he can discover for himself. Jesus answered the lawyer's first question by asking him another question. He held his ground. He was leading this man to discover truth for himself, in a novel way, and in a way that he would remember.

The lawyer found himself rattling off the answer to his own question, like a school kid reciting, and apparently he was embarrassed. This wasn't working out the way he had anticipated. So he tried again to take the discussion to an intellectual plane where he could compete. He came up with another question. Verse 29, "But he, willing to justify himself, said unto Jesus, And who is my neighbour?"

Who was one's neighbor was a common question in those days. The Jewish people were not exactly neighborly. In fact, they were known to be quite exclusive. They had long discussions about who should be associated with, and who should be avoided, and the list of ones to avoid was always the longer.

Jesus responded to the lawyer's question by telling a story, beginning with verse 30. "And Jesus answering said, A certain man went down from Jerusalem to Jericho, and fell among thieves, which stripped him of his raiment, and wounded him, and departed, leaving him half dead. And by chance there came down a certain priest that way: and when he saw him, he passed by on the other side. And likewise a Levite, when he was at the place, came and looked on him, and passed by on the other side. But a certain Samaritan, as he journeyed, came where he was: and when he saw him, he had compassion on him, and went to him, and bound up his wounds, pouring in oil and wine, and set him on his own beast, and brought him to an inn, and took care of him [apparently all night, for] . . . on the morrow when he departed, he took out two pence, and gave them to the host, and said unto him, Take care of him; and whatsoever thou spendest more, when I come again, I will repay thee."

Then Jesus asked the lawyer, "Which now of these, thinkest thou, was neighbour unto him that fell among thieves? And he said, He that showed mercy on him." He didn't want to use the word *Samaritan*.

Then said Jesus unto him, "Go and do thou likewise." End of story. Was that really the end of the story? Do you hear a story like the one about the Good Samaritan and find yourself able to go and do likewise? Or was Jesus sending this lawyer to his knees?

Good Samaritans aren't made by starting a Good Samaritan Club and deliberately choosing to be compassionate. Instead, they are good Samaritans because they can't help it. The only way this lawyer, who could not even take the name Samaritan on his lips, was to become loving and compassionate, was for him to go to his knees and become acquainted with the One that Jesus represented.

Put Yourself in the Picture

The best way to personalize a Bible story such as this is to put yourself in the picture. When you read about the thief on the cross, *you're* the thief on the cross. When you read about the blind man by the side of the road, *you're* blind Bartimaeus crying out, "Jesus, thou son of David, have mercy on me." So when you study the story of the good Samaritan, *you're* the good Samaritan. . . . No you're not! And I'm not either! At worst, we're the ones who beat him up in the first place. And at best, we're the one who was beaten up.

So you are the man, traveling from Jerusalem to Jericho. It's a trip of about twenty miles. Jerusalem stood at a higher elevation, so you are walking downhill. You walk briskly, for this is not a safe place to loiter. This is a place that has recesses and caves, where thieves and robbers lurk and frequently waylay travelers, as you well know. You go down through a narrow ravine, known as the Valley of Blood, and the inevitable happens. A group of armed men attack you from behind. You haven't a chance even to defend yourself. They take your money and your watch and even your clothes. And then, as if that were not enough, they mug you and finally leave you unconscious, weltering in your own blood.

You lie there for a long time. Finally you come to. The sun is hot. You try to move, but find you are unable to get up. You groan and struggle, but it's no use. But there's good news. You see the preacher coming. Surely the preacher will help. But he doesn't even slow down. He passes by on the other side of the road and barely glances in your direction.

Don't Blame the Preacher

Don't be too hard on the preacher! He may have been late and was hurrying to deliver a sermon at the synagogue in Jericho. Maybe he was even planning to preach on brotherly love. If he hung around the Valley of Blood, where someone had already been done in by the robbers, the same thing might happen to him. It would certainly be the lesser of two evils to leave the man and hurry on to Jericho. The spiritual need of his parishioners certainly should come before the needs of *one* man who was probably going to die anyway. Surely the priest must have done some rationalizing like this, as he hurried on his way.

You're getting chilled now. The sun has gone down behind an outcropping of rock, and you lie in the shadows. You're afraid it's all over for you, for not many travelers are on the road at this time of day. But good news! Here comes the church treasurer! He not only can help you to safety, but perhaps he can pay for your medical bills and even get you some clothes. Hope rises in your heart as you see him come over to where you are.

You try to speak, but your words only come out as a groan. Your lips are parched; you can hardly move. He looks down at you and then glances quickly around to see if robbers are lurking nearby. And he hurries on toward town.

Of course he must hurry on. He's carrying a bag filled with the offering money. It wouldn't be right to risk losing the Lord's money by staying in a place like this. Furthermore, his wife and children are expecting him, and running the risk of getting beaten up and robbed on the Jericho Road would not be the fatherly thing to do. He must have thought it through carefully as he hurried on his way, pausing now and again to glance back over his shoulder to make sure he wasn't being followed.

It looks hopeless now. You struggle again to move, but find you are too weak. You are left dizzy and short of breath from even the attempt. It's almost dark, and you are chilled to the bone. You try to resign yourself to slowly losing consciousness and giving in to the inevitable. Even if another traveler comes this way, he wouldn't be likely to see you there, off the side of the road in the shadows.

But you hear footsteps! Can it be possible? You strain your eyes to catch a glimpse of someone approaching—and your heart sinks. Oh! It's a Samaritan. You know how things are between the Jews and the Samaritans. You know how you have treated Samaritans yourself in the past. And you shrink back inside yourself, knowing that if your roles were reversed, you not only would not help him, you would probably spit in his face.

Who Could Believe It?

The Samaritan slows down. He sees you. You brace yourself for the worst. But he comes closer. He speaks gently to you. "What happened? You're hurt! Let me help you." You can't believe it. He touches you, carefully examining you so as to cause you the least pain possible. He comes close. He begins to bind up your wounds, pouring on the oil and wine. He feels your clammy skin and realizes how cold you are. He takes off his own garment, in spite of the coolness of the evening, and wraps you in its warmth. And then kindly and tenderly he helps you onto his donkey and takes you to the closest inn, all the while encouraging you to hope for a full recovery.

As you sink back into the warmth and comfort of the bed provided for you at the good Samaritan's expense, you can hardly believe your good fortune. He cares for you all through the long night, and in the morning, when you are feeling stronger, you hear him make arrangements for you to rest there as long as necessary—*at his expense!* You think about your family and friends and know they will never believe it when you tell them—but you can hardly wait to share the good news of what happened to you on the road to Jericho.

Look Who the Good Samaritan Is!

Let's redo the story now, with the most exciting part, because this is the story of Jesus. Long ago, the father of our race went down—way down. He went down from a Garden, with two trees, and his wife went with him. They went down, and the race has been going down ever since, degenerating in physical strength, mental power, and moral worth. The thief and robber who stripped them of their garments of light had gone down before them, down from the heavenly courts. He wounded them and left them for dead. The wounded victims tried to stitch fig leaves together to replace the garments he had taken from them. But it didn't work. And the human race is still on that downward path.

Then the Good Samaritan came. By chance? No, He planned it. He came on purpose. He saw us and had pity on us. He left His home, the safety of His beautiful home, to come down to this world of trouble. He came in contact with us. He touched the untouchables. He is touched with the feelings of our infirmities. He put His robe around us, sacrificing His own life to save ours. He poured in oil and wine, the oil of the Holy Spirit and the wine of His own shed blood. With His stripes we are healed.

And then He takes us to the inn. Do you know where it is? There's one in your town! It may be a simple building, or it may have steeples and stained glass. But it's there. And He gives instruction to the innkeepers. If you haven't found yourself in the story yet, you'd better now! For He says to the innkeepers, "Take care of him. Take care of him, and when I come again, I will repay you." And now you are one of the innkeepers!

The Good Samaritan doesn't just stop by once and then disappear. He's coming back! And He's promised, "When I come again, I will repay you."

Chapter 4
The Prodigal Sons

He lived in his father's house through his growing-up years. Now all of that seemed long ago. It was a slow process, almost imperceptible, that took him from being the trusting child, holding on to his father's hand as they walked out to do the chores, looking at his father with love and respect, and finding joy in companionship with his father to a son who wanted to leave home. But now all had changed. Now he resented his father's restraints, chafed at his counsel, and detested his instructions. For a time he lived as a prodigal at home, but now he wanted out. His father seemed severe, exacting, unreasonable. Then one day he came up with a plan.

He went to his father and boldly asked for his share of the inheritance. He knew he would need these blessings in order to make it comfortably on his own. He wasn't foolish enough to simply run away, but in essence, he said, "Drop dead, Dad." He wanted no further relationship with his father, except to spend his father's money.

According to this parable, in Luke 15:13, it wasn't long after that he left. It says, "Not many days after the younger son gathered all together, and took his journey into a far country, and there wasted his substance with riotous living."

So the first step of independence from his father, even while a member of his father's household, and the second step of leaving his father's house and heading for the far country, were not far separated.

There in the far country, the son abandoned all judgment and reason and restraint. He didn't budget his money; he didn't invest it. He certainly didn't work to earn more. He just spent it unthinkingly.

Occasionally one of his friends would ask about his family. "What's your father like?"

"Oh, he's stern, unbending, exacting. Really strict. Can't ever please him."

"What about your older brother?"

"He's a drag. Always out in the fields before sunup. Always trying to please the old man. Let's talk about something else."

But the younger prodigal had too many friends—the wrong kind. When he ran out of money, his friends left and things got hard, there in the far country. "When he had spent all, there arose a mighty famine in that land; and he began to be in want." Luke 15:14.

This was a new experience. The friends he thought he had didn't know him now. He was hungry for the first time in his life. He was ragged and tattered. And he did what prodigals have done for centuries. He began trying to save himself from the mess he had gotten himself into. He went to work, hoping to get his act together and satisfy his immediate and urgent needs.

Gradually he came to the end of his meager resources. His money was gone; his topcoat had been pawned off long ago. He had sold his suit and vest, and even his shirt. And finally, it says, "he came to himself." He not only realized a need, but he realized his own helplessness. That's what happened to him there in the pigpen. And when that happened, his attitude toward his father began to change.

He began to think how his father treated his servants. His father was a far kinder master than the one he now worked for. The servants in his father's house had plenty to eat and decent clothes and a place to live. He looked around the pigpen with disgust. "My father's servants are better off than this," he told himself. And a plan began to form in his mind.

As he came to himself, he also began to come to his father. He still underestimated his father's love and acceptance. But he no longer saw his father as a tyrant. And he planned a speech. He will go back home and ask to be taken on as a servant. Who knows? maybe his father would even give him special consideration.

Then he gave up trying to fix up his own life. He didn't wait to save money for some new clothes or a donkey to ride home. He immediately arose and headed for his father's house. And wonder of wonders, before he even got to the gate, his father came running to meet him. His father, with aching heart, has been watching down the road, day after day. His father has been yearning for his return, and when he saw him coming afar off, he ran to meet him. Love is of keen sight.

The son began his carefully rehearsed speech, but never got a chance to even finish it. He said, "I have sinned." His father put his own robe around him to cover his shame. He said, "I am no more worthy." His father put his ring on his finger, reinstating him in the family. He had planned to ask a servant's place, but he never had a chance, for his father put shoes on his feet—the servants didn't wear shoes in those days. He was accepted and established fully as his father's son. And in place of the husks that the pigs had fed upon, he is now feasting from the bounties at his father's table.

The Second Prodigal

"Now his elder son was in the field: and as he came and drew nigh to the house, he heard musick and dancing. And he called one of the servants, and asked what these things meant. And he said unto him, Thy brother is come; and thy father hath killed the fatted calf, because he hath received him safe and sound. And he was angry, and would not go in: therefore came his father out, and intreated him. And he answering said to his father, Lo, these many years do I serve thee, neither transgressed I at any time thy commandment: and yet thou never gavest me a kid, that I might make merry with my friends: but as soon as this thy son was come, which hath devoured thy living with harlots, thou hast killed for him the fatted calf. And he said unto him, Son, thou art ever with me, and all that I have is thine. It was meet that we should make merry, and be glad: for this thy brother was dead, and is alive again; and was lost, and is found." Verses 25-32.

Which prodigal son do you identify with? This father had not one, but two of them, didn't he? The second prodigal thought he had done well in keeping the commandments, for he says, "Neither transgressed I at any time thy commandment." But his obedience was a legal obedience only, and as such was worth nothing. The one who attempts to keep the commandments of God from a sense of obligation merely, because he is required to do so, will never enter into the joy of obedience. He does not obey. Obedience is a matter of the heart, not merely the outward actions.

The elder brother gave evidence here that he was a prodigal at heart, even though outwardly he was still in his father's house. He was in a far country on the inside, and hadn't even progressed as far as the pigpen!

The elder brother was a "good liver". But it isn't much fun being good in the way he was good. That kind of good living will put ulcers in your stomach and lines on your face, because badness held in check is not goodness, and never will be. Sitting on a keg of dynamite that is about ready to explode is a terrible experience, more terrible the longer you sit there. And things finally exploded the day of the feast. All of the hostility the elder brother had held in came to the surface.

He had watched in silence for years as his father spent time looking down the road with his binoculars, instead of looking at the good job his elder son was doing in the field. He had wanted his father to forget about his younger brother. In his mind, his younger brother was as good as dead, and even when his father came out from the feast to reason with him, he referred to him contemptuously as "this thy son" instead of "my brother."

But is the father unequal in his concern for his two prodigal sons? No, as soon as he realized the distance the older son has put between them, he goes out to meet him too. He doesn't give up on the elder son, even though he was being unreasonable. The father loved both of his boys and did everything he could to reach both of them.

The father had made provision for the younger brother, in

the robe and the shoes and the ring and the feast. And he made provision for the older brother as well. Have you been a prodigal like the younger son? There is forgiveness and acceptance and the robe of His righteousness waiting for you and a place of fellowship for you at His table. Have you been a prodigal like the elder son? Hear the Father's voice saying, "All that I have is thine." His forgiveness and acceptance and robe of righteousness and the fellowship with Him at His table is for you too!

Won't you join in the feast provided? It doesn't matter which of the prodigal sons you have been imitating. All that the Father has is for you, and is yours, if you accept it. The Father has come out to meet you and invites you into His family today.

Chapter 5
Of Such Is the Kingdom of Heaven

Have you ever read the poem about the six blind men and the elephant? It tells of six men who wanted to find out what an elephant was like, but they had a problem. They couldn't see it. So each of them approached the elephant, grabbed on to the first thing they could reach, and formed their conclusions on the basis of what they experienced.

One caught hold of the tail, and said, "An elephant is very like a rope." A second found an ear, and said, "An elephant is very like a fan." Another touched one of the elephant's legs and said, "An elephant is very like a tree." And yet another stumbled against the elephant's broad side and insisted, "An elephant is very like a wall. " And so it went.

They had a lot of discussion and argument, each loudly insisting his conclusion was correct. And the poem ends, saying, "Though all were partly in the right, they all were in the wrong!"

How do you describe something you can't see? It's hard, isn't it? The only way to begin is to seek for comparisons. And by making many comparisons, a picture begins to emerge.

In making analogies and parables, it's important to remember the blind men and the elephant, and not to make the mistake they made of thinking that one picture says it all. When Jesus came to this earth and began to try to describe the kingdom of heaven to people who had never seen it, He employed parables. It took a lot of parables. No one could say it all. But each parable added a dimension of understanding to fill out the picture.

Let's look at some of His mini-parables and try to find out

more about the kingdom of righteousness that He tried to portray. When Jesus spoke of His kingdom, He was talking about one of two things, either the kingdom of grace, or God's work of grace in the human heart. So each of His parables about the kingdom of grace gives us further insights into His righteousness, which comes by faith in Him. Watch for it as we proceed.

The Grain of Mustard Seed (Matthew 13:31, 32)

"Another parable put he forth unto them, saying, The kingdom of heaven is like to a grain of mustard seed, which a man took, and sowed in his field: which indeed is the least of all seeds: but when it is grown, it is the greatest among herbs, and becometh a tree, so that the birds of the air come and lodge in the branches thereof."

What can we learn about the kingdom of heaven in comparing it to a grain of mustard seed? Well, it starts out small, and then grows. Zechariah 4:10 asks, "Who hath despised the day of small things?" It's an easy thing for us to do, isn't it? But God often works through what might appear to be insignificant. We are often in danger of missing the still, small voice in our search for the wind and the fire.

Yet just because the beginning is small doesn't mean that it stops there. The results are as big as eternity. Jesus knew this and worked on that principle in His dealings with Nicodemus. He planted the seed in the heart and then waited. For a long time there were no apparent results. But in the end, Nicodemus became one of the trees of righteousness, the planting of the Lord.

That's how it works, in salvation by faith in Him. The seed may be small, but the harvest is sure, as we give the Lord time to work in our lives.

The Leaven (Matthew 13:33)

"Another parable spake he unto them; The kingdom of heaven is like unto leaven, which a woman took, and hid in three measures of meal, till the whole was leavened."

God's work of grace in the heart is unseen. It works from the inside out, not from the outside in. God knows that when you make bread, you put the yeast on the inside, and then wait for it to do its work. You don't make the bread and then sprinkle yeast across the top and expect it to rise.

The plan of beginning on the outside and trying to work toward the inside has always failed, and always will fail. God's plan with you is to begin at the very seat of all difficulties, the heart, and then from out of the heart will issue the principles of righteousness; the reformation will be outward as well as inward.

Do you want to know if God is working in your life? You won't always be able to tell by looking at the outward manifestations. You can only know if you are accepting the leaven of His grace in your heart on a daily basis. As His grace is received into the heart, the results are inevitable, even though they may not be seen immediately.

As the leaven, when mingled with the meal, works from the inside to the outside, so it is by the renewing of the heart that the grace of God works to transform the life. No mere external change is sufficient to bring us into harmony with God. There are many who try to reform by correcting this or that bad habit, and they hope in this way to become Christians, but they are beginning in the wrong place. The first work must be with the heart.

The parable of the ten bridesmaids in Matthew 25 brings out the same truth. It was not enough that they had lamps—external goodness. In order to be admitted to the wedding, it was essential that they have oil—the Holy Spirit in the heart. It is what's on the inside that counts in the kingdom of heaven, not the externals.

First the Blade, Then the Ear (Mark 4:26-29)

"And he said, So is the kingdom of God, as if a man should cast seed into the ground; and should sleep, and rise night and day, and the seed should spring and grow up, he knoweth not how. For the earth bringeth forth fruit of herself; first the blade, then the ear, and after that the full corn in the ear. But when the fruit is brought forth, immediately he putteth in the sickle, because the harvest is come."

We can help in sowing the seed, but *we* don't make the seed grow. The growing of the seed is God's work. Suppose a man should cast seed into the ground and then try to stay awake to help it grow. Suppose he sat out by his garden plot and kept an eye on things. Why he would fall asleep before the first radish sprout made it to the surface, wouldn't he?

The farmer's job is to sow the seed, to give it regular water and cultivation, and then *leave it alone*. God takes care of the rest of the process.

We aren't expected to watch ourselves, constantly checking ourselves to see if we are producing fruit. Our part is to sow the seed. And remember what the seed represents—it is the Word of God. We study God's Word for ourselves, we accept Him into our lives day by day, and then we let Him do His work. We may not understand how He does it, but this doesn't matter. What's important is that we understand how to do the work assigned to us.

Over and over again we are reminded that there is a process involved. It takes time to grow. It takes time for the leaven to do its work. Even after the plant has surfaced, even after the seed is no longer hidden in the earth, it still takes time. First comes the blade, then the ear, and after that the full corn in the ear.

We hate this delay! We want instant righteousness, *now*— yesterday if possible. We want it prepackaged, just add water— kind of in the same way we can have instant soup or instant oatmeal. Waiting is not our idea of a fun way to spend time. Yet the very waiting process which we find so distasteful is in itself of value. It shows us where our weaknesses lie. It shows us what our priorities really are. It shows us ourselves and our deep need of the grace God offers. The waiting develops the fruits of the Spirit in our lives, even while we chafe at the time factor involved.

But God knows how to do His work, in nature as well as in human hearts. He has built in the time factor as the very best way in which He can do His work. We cooperate with Him as we accept His time frame instead of trying to force Him to accept ours. And although it takes time, the results are sure and certain so long as we stay with Him.

Treasure Hid in a Field (Matthew 13:44)

"Again, the kingdom of heaven is like unto treasure hid in a field; the which when a man hath found, he hideth, and for joy thereof goeth and selleth all that he hath, and buyeth that field."

The Pearl of Great Price (Matthew 13:45, 46)

"Again, the kingdom of heaven is like unto a merchant man, seeking goodly pearls: who, when he had found one pearl of great price, went and sold all that he had, and bought it."

These two parables are similar and offer an interesting picture of the kingdom of God. After repeatedly teaching that salvation is free, that whosoever will may come, that we have nothing to bring except our great need, all of a sudden Jesus tells us that the kingdom of heaven has to be bought. How do we explain this?

Have you ever tried to give something to a child whose hands were full? Have you ever smiled as you saw their eyes light up and heard their squeals of delight at the sight of what you had to offer? And then have you watched their dilemma as they try to decide what to do? They realize they can't take what you are offering them until they let go of what they already have. And sometimes it takes a struggle to decide which is more important!

That's the way it is in the kingdom of God. No matter what you have that you are depending on, you must let go of it before you can receive the treasure of heaven. It is essential that you "sell" all you have. Are you rich? Are you intelligent? Are you well educated? Are you talented? Are you good looking? Are you capable? No matter where your strengths lie, you will only be strong in reality when you realize your weakness. Your only hope is still in accepting the gifts that Jesus has to offer. And so long as you hang onto "all" that you have, no matter what that all includes, you cannot accept His priceless treasure.

The kingdom of heaven is free, yet it costs everything. It cost Jesus everything. He held nothing back as He came the full length of the road that reached from His house to ours. He did not spare himself. And as we accept His free salvation, we can hold nothing back. If we do, we will find our hands full of our own baubles and toys and be unable to reach out to accept what He has to offer.

Of Such Is the Kingdom of Heaven (Mark 10:13-15)

"They brought young children to him, that he should touch them: and his disciples rebuked those that brought them. But when Jesus saw it, he was much displeased, and said unto them, Suffer the little children to come unto me, and forbid them not: for of such is the kingdom of God. Verily I say unto you, Whosoever shall not receive the kingdom of God as a little child, he shall not enter therein."

What is it about little children that appeals to us? What can we learn from them about the way to the kingdom of heaven? Well, first of all, little children are helpless. They are dependent. They need the protection of someone who is stronger and wiser than they are.

In this life, we expect our children to grow from dependence to independence. If we are wise parents, we encourage them in their reaching out to learn so that they can grow and become capable. We don't want them to stay dependent upon us forever. We know that if they continue to be helpless and dependent, something has gone wrong in their development.

But in God's kingdom, it's just the opposite. We start out thinking we can handle things on our own. We start out independent, and He has to lead us through the painful process of realizing our helplessness, our need of complete dependence upon Him. Perhaps this is why Jesus specified *little* children as being the ones to use as our examples.

There's another thing about little children. They haven't

been around long enough to develop a track record. They come to us with their needs because they have needs. They don't come with a long list of the good things they have done for us as reasons why we should give them our help. It is enough that we have the help to give and they need the help we have.

And that's the way it is with God. It isn't what we've done to deserve or merit His help that motivates Him to save us. Our great need is our greatest argument, now and always. It isn't what we have done for Him. It's what we need for Him to do for us.

Little children are not afraid to love. They haven't become hardened through years of fear of rejection and pain and disappointment. They love openly and trustingly and expectantly. How easy it is to reach children with the love of Jesus. When He was here on this earth, the children came to Him gladly. They shouted His praises. It was the older folk who held back and questioned and rejected the evidences of His love for them.

The seed and the leaven and the growing corn and the hidden treasure and the pearl and the little children—all are pictures of the kingdom of God. Each one by itself is inadequate. No parable could say it all. But taken all together, we begin to understand the message of Jesus as it relates to the nature of His kingdom and how we may enter into it.

Chapter 6
The Heavenly Pay Scale

It happened at a church-sponsored school. The school was situated in Brooklyn. The students were encouraged to become involved in what they called "progressive class work"—completing certain lists of activities and learning certain skills for each grade level. Those of us in the first grade had been studying hard all year to get our Sunbeam and Busy Bee pins and scarves. The older students had worked to become Friends and Comrades and Master Comrades. (This was before we had heard about Russian communism!)

And so the night of the investiture came, when we were to receive our awards. I looked at the table where the youth director had laid out all of the certificates and pins and scarves, and I saw I was to receive a small green kerchief for my work. The older students were to receive larger kerchiefs with shiny plastic sliders. But we first graders had to tie a knot in our scarves to keep them together!

I had studied hard for my award and felt rather disappointed at what I was getting in return. I remember smiling desperately at the youth director, hoping he would notice me and feel sorry for me and maybe give me at least one of those plastic sliders! But it didn't work. That evening I discovered the painful truth that in this world you work for what you get, and you get what you worked for. And that's the way it is. One by one we went forward and received our awards, and the meeting was about over when someone had a bright idea. My father and uncle were evangelists, holding meetings in downtown New York City, and someone said, "Why, these preachers must have learned all of these things that the Master Comrades know. Why don't we invest them right now—and their wives too?"

So my father and mother and uncle and aunt went forward and were invested as Master Comrades. And I knew good and well they hadn't even done the requirements for Sunbeams and Busy Bees!

I was not the least bit happy about the honor given to my parents that night. I still loved my parents, you understand, but I wasn't at all sure about the youth director. In fact, I felt so deeply about the experience that it set back my interest in progressive class work by at least twenty years. I didn't realize until years later that Jesus told a story that was very similar to that investiture service.

It's found in Matthew 20:1-4. "The kingdom of heaven is like unto a man that is an householder, which went out early in the morning to hire labourers into his vineyard. And when he had agreed with the labourers for a penny a day, he sent them into his vineyard. And he went out about the third hour [or 9:00 a.m.], and saw others standing idle in the marketplace, and said unto them; Go ye also into the vineyard, and whatsoever is right I will give you. And they went their way."

Apparently they trusted him, for he did not specify the amount of remuneration. "Again he went out about the sixth and ninth hour [which would be 12:00 noon and 3:00 in the afternoon], and did likewise. And about the eleventh hour [5:00 p.m.] he went out, and found others standing idle, and saith unto them, Why stand ye here all the day idle? They say unto him, Because no man hath hired us. He saith unto them, Go ye also into the vineyard; and whatsoever is right, that shall ye receive." Verses 5-7.

Well, one thing is sure. You're not going to earn much going to work at 5:00 in the afternoon, one hour before quitting time. But at the very least, maybe they could fill their pockets with some grapes to take home for supper. And so they went willingly to the vineyard.

"When even was come, the lord of the vineyard saith unto his steward, Call the labourers, and give them their hire, beginning from the last unto the first. And when they came that were hired about the eleventh hour, they received every man a penny." Verses 8, 9.

We may not be too impressed with the "penny" described in the King James Version. Inflation has made pennies so worthless that people hardly bother to pick them up off the street anymore. But in Jesus' day a penny was a day's wage. The workers who had been hired at the eleventh hour were astonished.

The workers who had been there all day were astonished too. Their hopes began to rise, and they could hardly wait for their turn to come to the pay master's table. "But when the first came, they supposed that they should have received more; and they likewise received every man a penny. And when they had received it, they murmured against the goodman of the house, saying, These last have wrought but one hour, and thou hast made them equal unto us, which have borne the burden and heat of the day.

"But he answered one of them, and said, Friend, I do thee no wrong: didst not thou agree with me for a penny? Take that thine is, and go thy way: I will give unto this last, even as unto thee. Is it not lawful for me to do what I will with mine own? Is thine eye evil, because I am good? So the last shall be first, and the first last: for many be called, but few chosen." Verses 10-16.

Well, this is indeed a strange story, isn't it? We understand that the vineyard owner represents God, and that makes it even more strange. Yes, we can agree, it's lawful for Him to do what He pleases with His own. Since all things belong to Him, it's all right for Him to be generous. But why did He discriminate against the ones who had worked such long hours? If He wants to give His gifts to those who don't deserve it, why stop with the one-hour workers? Why not give everybody ten pennies or a hundred? It looks as if He's being generous to some and not to others. And that makes us uncomfortable.

The Penny

The secret to understanding this parable is found in the secret of what the penny represents. What are the wages that are paid to the workers for God? Are they given advantages and blessings here in this life? Are they given a mansion of gold or stars in their crown or a special place in the kingdom of heaven to come? And if this is the case, why wouldn't it be best to hold out until the last possible minute before joining God's service, so as to experience His generosity instead of feeling shortchanged?

It's quite obvious that God operates on a different value system than we do. But since that is true, we'd better take advantage of the opportunity given us in this parable to understand a little more about His system. If we are unhappy with His method of payment now, we will certainly be unhappy later on too.

So what is the reward? What is the penny? It is Jesus Himself! He can't give the twelve-hour workers more than the one-hour workers, because He can give neither more nor less than Himself. Why? Because in giving Himself He gives all the riches of the universe.

When you have seen that, you realize that, in a sense, the twelve-hour workers received more than the one-hour workers after all. For while the one-hour workers were standing idle in the marketplace, the twelve-hour workers had had the privilege of a full day of fellowship and companionship working with the owner of the vineyard.

If you think that the reward is heaven at last and perhaps more stars in your crown or a bigger mansion, you will be disappointed. But when you realize that the reward is Jesus and that heaven itself can offer nothing more, nothing greater, then your reward begins when you enter His service—because through Jesus we enter into rest, heaven begins here.

We respond to His invitation, "Come, learn of Me," and in thus coming we begin the life eternal. Heaven is a ceaseless approaching to God through Christ. The longer we are in the heaven of bliss, the more and still more of glory will be opened to us; and the more we know of God, the more intense will be our happiness.

In Matthew 19 Jesus meets the rich young ruler who came

running after Him, wanting to know what to do to enter into life. And Jesus said, "Keep the commandments." He was trying to smoke him out of the woods. "Keep the commandments."

"I have."

"What about this one?"

"Uh oh. I'm in trouble."

The man went away sorrowful. The disciples stood by, watching and thinking, "Here is a rich man who refuses to follow Jesus. He is going away sorrowful. That is too bad. But we have chosen to follow Jesus. Therefore we are right, and he is wrong."

Peter, who was usually the spokesman, got his mouth working first and blurted out, "Too bad for him, Lord. He left. But what about us? We are following you. What are we going to get out of it?"

Peter was operating on our system of values, wasn't he? "What are we going to get?" I think that if I had been Jesus, I would have said, "You disciples get out of my sight. Give me another twelve and let me start over again. After three years, you still haven't gotten the message."

Instead, Jesus met them where they were. Verse 28. "Jesus said unto them, Verily I say unto you, that ye which have followed me, in the regeneration when the Son of man shall sit in the throne of his glory, ye also shall sit upon twelve thrones, judging the twelve tribes of Israel."

Can't you see the disciples, excited about the good news of the reward they would receive for following Jesus?

But then Jesus went on and added something else. "And every one that hath forsaken houses, or brethren, or sisters, or father, or mother, or wife, or children, or lands, for my name's sake, shall receive an hundredfold," and Mark adds, "Now in this time," and "in the world to come eternal life." Mark 10:30.

Since the reward is Jesus Himself, the reward begins here and now—a hundredfold. And the reward at the end of the day is simply a continuation of the experience already begun. The rewards *in* service are just as meaningful as the rewards *for* service. Fellowship with Jesus is the highest reward that can be given.

Those who are unwilling to stand all the day idle and who are more interested in service and fellowship with Jesus than in the rewards that may be given will find in the end that the reward will be enough, and more than enough.

Chapter 7
The Race for the Kingdom

Have you ever run in a race? I guess most of us have at one time or another. I remember one race particularly. It was a very important race, because they were giving away a free car, and I was desperately interested in winning that car. I was six years old, and the car was a toy. But I ran as fast as I could, and I won the car. I played with it on the living room floor for a long time after that.

Then there was the race during a college picnic, where we had tandem bicycles, and the fellows were steering, and the girls were helping in the engine room behind. I was so concerned about winning that race that the girl and I started off too fast, and her feet left the pedals and never got back on the pedals the whole race. I didn't know why everyone was laughing as we crossed the finish line, but we won!

We are all in a race today—the race for the kingdom. And Jesus told a parable about this race for the kingdom in Matthew 21:28-32: "But what think ye? A certain man had two sons; and he came to the first, and said, Son, go work to day in my vineyard. He answered and said, I will not: but afterward he repented, and went. And he came to the second, and said likewise. And he answered and said, I go, sir: and went not. Whether of them twain did the will of his father? They say unto him, the first. Jesus saith unto them, Verily I say unto you, That the publicans and the harlots go into the kingdom of God before you. For John came unto you in the way of righteousness, and ye believed him not: but the publicans and the harlots believed him: and ye, when ye had seen it, repented not afterward, that ye might believe him."

This parable presents two classes of people. The first group are the ones who make no profession, but who end up working in the vineyard. They end up in the kingdom of heaven. The second group make a great profession, but they stop right there. And in the end, the kingdom is taken away from them.

Jesus described this second group in yet another of His vineyard parables. Those who were supposed to be the keepers of the vineyard killed not only the servants of the vineyard owner, but his own son as well. And after they had killed the heir, the command was given, "The kingdom of God shall be taken from you, and given to a nation bringing forth the fruits thereof." Matthew 21:43.

The news about the kingdom is good news for publicans and harlots, but it can be bad news for religious people who have felt secure in their morality and have never recognized their great need for something more than simply to make a profession. To say, "I go, sir," is not enough.

To try to discover more about this strange kingdom that admits publicans and harlots and yet closes its door to the "good" people, let's look at one of Jesus' own disciples, Matthew, who was a tax collector. "As Jesus passed forth from thence, he saw a man, named Matthew, sitting at the receipt of custom: and he saith unto him, Follow me. And he arose, and followed him." Matthew 9:9.

My, that was sudden, wasn't it? Matthew must have been surprised at the invitation, but he did not hesitate. You read the inspired commentary and you find that Matthew had already heard of Jesus. His heart had been touched, and he had been convicted of sin. He was a cheat and a liar. Publicans were known for this. That's the way they made their living—ripping people off. But beneath the unpromising exterior, Matthew was open to the gospel about the kingdom. However, he didn't think there was the ghost of a chance for him to enter the race. He was painfully aware of the gap between his own lifestyle and that of the Jewish leaders whom he supposed to be as righteous as they were moral. So he never thought that he would receive

4438

an invitation to enter the race, until the day he heard the friendly words of Jesus, "Follow me."

Matthew left everything and followed. This was the chance of a lifetime. It was what he wanted more than anything else.

Word went around town concerning what had happened to Matthew. Other publicans and sinners dared to hope. And when Matthew had a feast and invited all his friends, they came eagerly to listen to this Jesus. Matthew didn't have any righteous friends. They were all publicans and sinners, just like himself. But this was the opportunity Jesus had been longing for, and He did not hesitate to accept, in spite of what He knew the priests and rulers would think of such a gathering.

Verses 10-13: "Behold, many publicans and sinners came and sat down with him and his disciples. And when the Pharisees saw it, they said unto his disciples, Why eateth your Master with publicans and sinners? But when Jesus heard that, he said unto them, They that be whole need not a physician, but they that are sick, But go ye and learn what that meaneth, I will have mercy, and not sacrifice: for I am not come to call the righteous, but sinners to repentance."

What is Jesus saying here? He is saying that no one is going to be really interested in the good news about the kingdom until he realizes his great need.

One time a young man from the state college in California came to some meetings my dad was holding. He was a distance runner, and he was good. He kept coming to the meetings, and the Spirit of God spoke to his heart. He was convicted concerning the Sabbath and all the rest of it, and he was struggling, trying to decide what to do.

Hebrews 12:1 talks about the race for the kingdom, and says, "Let us lay aside every weight, and the sin which doth so easily beset us, and let us run with patience the race that is set before us." This young man was being convicted that he should become involved in a race with far bigger stakes than the prizes in the earthly races he had entered up until that time. But he was not certain it was worth the sacrifice.

About that time there was a race scheduled for Sabbath. It was a distance race, his specialty. He went to the race and started running. He was way ahead of the rest. But the harder he ran, the more he kept thinking about the seventh day being the Sabbath. He was in the last quarter of the race when suddenly he stopped and walked away. He went home and kept the rest of that Sabbath. His decision was made. He had finally recognized his greatest need was to win in the race for the kingdom, and he became involved in the right race.

The Jewish leaders who condemned Jesus for associating with publicans and sinners did not understand this. They were involved in their own race, a race to get ahead of the next person in morality and standards and behavior. And the race for the kingdom didn't fit in with their plans.

No one is motivated to enter a race if he thinks he has already won. The Jewish leaders thought they had already won. They were self-satisfied. Were they not the chosen people? Didn't they pay tithe and fast and attend church faithfully? Didn't they offer their long prayers at the appointed hours? Didn't they wash before meals? Didn't they make the proper sacrifices in the temple? The Bible says time and again that the people just before the second coming of Christ will be very similar to the ones who were living when He came the first time. So it is possible that there are people today who find the message about the race for the kingdom unnecessary. Could there be some of us today who think we have already attained and have no need to enter the race?

Let's add one more text to this study, Luke 7:1-10. In this passage we see the man who had asked for Jesus to come and heal his servant. He was a Roman army officer, a centurion. The Jewish leaders had come to Jesus with a request from him, and they added, "He is worthy, for he built us a synagogue." He deserves your attention. He merits what you can give him.

Jesus started out toward the centurion's home, but when the centurion heard that Jesus was coming, he sent word back to Jesus saying, "I am not worthy. I'm not even worthy for you to come under my roof."

Jesus was astonished at the faith of this man, and after commenting on what great faith he had, Jesus made this statement, "I say unto you, That many shall come from the east and west and shall sit down with Abraham, and Isaac, and Jacob, in the kingdom of heaven. But the children of the kingdom shall be cast out into outer darkness: there shall be weeping and gnashing of teeth." Matthew 8:11,12.

It says that those from the east and west come and sit down. What does that mean? Watchman Nee, in his book *Sit, Stand, Walk,* brings out the truth that to sit down in God's kingdom means to rest from labors, to cease from our own efforts to accomplish what only God can do.

This race for the kingdom is a sitting-down race! We can't even start it, much less finish it on our own. And that's a hard lesson to learn. Even for Abraham, Isaac, and Jacob, it came hard.

Abraham came from a far country. He and his wife Sarah had no children, and this was embarrassing. In those days, it was a status symbol to have at least one son. For a person whose name meant "Father of a multitude," "Mother of nations" that was hard to take. So Abraham and Sarah began running around, trying to help make things happen. And things happened all right. A son was produced—the wrong one. And he brought nothing but heartache and trouble. At this point Abraham and Sarah weren't even in the race.

Jacob didn't understand about a sitting-down race either. He had been promised a birthright, but it looked like the promise was not going to be fulfilled. Jacob began running around, trying to make it happen in his own strength, and he kept running for twenty years before one night at the brook when he finally understood how to enter the race for the kingdom.

Those who receive the prize in this race for the kingdom will have learned to sit down. They will have learned not to depend on their own efforts. They will have learned that "the race is not to the swift, nor the battle to the strong." They will learn that the race has already been won, and all they can do is to accept.

Does this mean we do nothing? No, this sitting down is extremely active! It involves not fighting when your instinct is to fight. The people of Israel had to do that, in their battle recorded in 2 Chronicles 20. They were told, "Ye shall not need to fight in this battle: set yourselves, stand ye still, and see the salvation of the Lord." Verse 17. It involves going forward at the very time when going forward seems the most impossible—not going forward to fight, but going forward in faith. The people of Israel had to learn that, too, at the Red Sea. They were surrounded by the enemy. Ahead was a sea that seemed impossible to cross, and Moses told them, in Exodus 14, "Fear ye not, stand still, and see the salvation of the Lord." "The Lord shall fight for you, and ye shall hold your peace." And then he said, "Go forward." Verses 13-15.

Why do the publicans and harlots go first, even ahead of the children of the kingdom? Because they find it easier to admit and realize their need. They have spent so much time fighting and knowing that they are losing, that they are willing to try another way. That is why they find it easier to give up and depend on the only One who can make it happen.

The children of the kingdom need to learn the same lesson, but at times the struggle is harder for them. And there will be some painful shifts at the very end, just before Jesus comes. Thousands who have thought they were children of the kingdom will walk away from the whole package, rather than humble themselves to accept salvation as a gift.

It happened after Matthew's feast; it is happening today. Thousands are making the same mistake as did the Pharisees whom Christ reproved. Such people trust in themselves. They do not realize their spiritual poverty. They insist on being saved in some way by performing some important work. And when they see that there is no way of weaving self into the work, they reject the salvation provided.

Will you accept the invitation today to enter the race for the kingdom—by accepting that which has already been won? Are you willing to join the publicans and the harlots and the sinners and those from the east and the west, and *sit down* in the kingdom of God?

Chapter 8
My Kingdom Is Not of This World

He was in Pilate's judgment hall. There had been no rest for Him that night. The death struggle in the Garden of Gethsemane had been followed by the kiss of betrayal. He had been pushed and shoved to the judgment hall and tried before Annas and then before Caiaphas. Now He stood before Pilate—weak, waffling Pilate—awaiting the outcome which He knew was inevitable. In fact, it was for this that He had come.

Pilate questioned Him about His kingdom. It was a strange kingdom in the eyes of the worldly ruler. Yet Jesus patiently and kindly tried to explain it to him. "My kingdom is not of this world," said Jesus. "If my kingdom were of this world, then would my servants fight, that I should not be delivered to the Jews: but now is my kingdom not from hence." John 18:36.

My kingdom is not of this world. If it were, *then* would my servants fight. That's hard truth to understand. It was hard for Pilate, and it's hard for us today. Jesus' own disciples had trouble understanding.

Peter missed it. He had a sword, and he wasn't afraid to use it. Although he wasn't particularly skillful, he didn't let that stand in his way! And yet, when Jesus submitted to be arrested by the mob in the Garden, Peter was the first disciple to turn tail and flee.

Peter was the one who urged Jesus to avoid the cross with its suffering and death, and for his efforts received one of the sternest rebukes Jesus ever gave. Peter was still fighting to save himself in the courtyard in the hall of Caiaphas. He struggled to save himself from embarrassment, from ridicule. He ended up denying Jesus in his attempt to save himself. He didn't understand that the servants of Jesus don't need to fight.

James and John didn't understand either. They came with their mother to seek the highest place in the kingdom. They were already among the closest three of Jesus' disciples. But it looked to them like there were going to be only two places of honor coming up—not three—one on the right hand, and the other on the left—and they wanted those places. They were fighting to get ahead of Peter, who would have been the other logical candidate, and so they made their request.

When the last journey to Jerusalem was undertaken, James and John were incensed at the refusal of the Samaritans to offer lodging and refreshment to Jesus and His disciples. They were ready to fight. They weren't sure they could handle things in a hand-to-hand combat with a whole village, so they requested some heavenly artillery to insure success. And they were surprised at the pained expression on Jesus' face when they asked for the fire. They didn't understand that the servants of Jesus don't need to fight.

Judas didn't understand either. He was the most intelligent of the disciples. He had picked up on things they had missed. But he didn't make it when it came to the part about not fighting. He was looking for a kingdom that *was* of this world. He considered Jesus too meek and mild and unassertive. He felt that Jesus should be a more aggressive leader. He figured Jesus needed a P.R. man, himself, for instance, to take charge of the strategy and direct the battle.

Judas tried to make it happen the day of the feeding of the five thousand. It was the perfect opportunity. The mood of the crowd was just right for raising a revolt. Jesus had outdone Himself in showing His divine authority by multiplying the loaves and the fishes. Judas couldn't believe it would all end by being sent off into the sunset in the smelly fishing boat, just as if nothing had happened.

Judas wanted to put Christ on the throne. He wanted to see

the kingdom established. But he wanted to do it through force, through fighting. And when Jesus did not cooperate with his plans, he decided to go underground.

And he came up with a clever plan. Well he knew the power of Jesus. He had not only seen it in action from the sidelines, he had felt that power in his own life, in healing the sick, cleansing the lepers, raising the dead, and casting out demons. He had no fears for the safety of Jesus. And he was tired of waiting.

The priests and rulers cooperated well. Judas had thought of everything. He made a special point to warn them to hold on tight, once they had Jesus in their grasp. Inwardly he laughed as he anticipated their surprise when Jesus disappeared into the crowd, as He had that day in Nazareth after the church service.

But things didn't go according to plan. Judas followed behind, waiting for the action to begin. But it didn't begin. And as the night wore away, a terrible fear began to gnaw at his heart. At last he realized that he had sold his Master to His death.

Suddenly a hoarse voice rang through the hall, "He is innocent; spare Him, O Caiaphas!"

Judas now pressed through the crowded courtroom. His face was pale and haggard, and great drops of sweat stood on his forehead. Rushing to the throne of judgment, he threw down before the high priest the pieces of silver that had been the price of his Lord's betrayal. Grasping the robe of Caiaphas, he begged him to release Jesus, saying He had done nothing worthy of death.

"I have sinned," cried Judas, "in that I have betrayed the innocent blood."

Judas did not understand about a kingdom for which you do not fight. And in the end, he fought himself into a corner, and a thin rope on a high branch was the only way out he could accept.

Have you ever fought to try to put Jesus on the throne in your life? Have you ever tried to fight your way in to the kingdom of heaven, the kingdom of grace?

We understand that Jesus would like to be on the throne of

our hearts, but we often misunderstand the method for placing Him on that throne. The kingdom of grace is a gift, and you don't fight for a gift.

This truth about the kingdom was stated to Pilate, right in the middle of the trial of Jesus, but it is just as true for today. It's easy to miss it. Don't overlook it. The person who is trying to fight sin and the devil is in the wrong kingdom. God's servants do not have to fight. God's servants are not supposed to fight. They are to allow Him to do their fighting through them.

If you have been struggling for years to overcome sin by gritting your teeth and trying hard and making resolutions, you're a victim of the kingdom of this world. If you've been working on your sins, trying to get your act together, you're a victim of the kingdom of this world. If you have missed the fact that salvation is a gift and that repentance is a gift and obedience is a gift, you're a victim of the kingdom of this world. This is hard truth for some to understand, and still harder to experience. But it's still good news, and I invite you to give it your careful study.

One time my father was holding public meetings in a particular town, and a prize fighter came and listened and became interested in the things of the kingdom. But he found it frustrating to try to deal with the sin problems in his life. And one day he told my father, "If the devil would just come out in the open, I could take a swing at him."

We're limited by our humanity. Even if the devil were not stronger and more powerful than we are, we still would not be able to fight him ourselves, for he is a spirit, and we aren't. And how can you fight a spirit? The only way would be to engage another Spirit to do your fighting for you.

We are invited to fight the fight of faith, the fight to set aside prime time every day for fellowship and communion with Jesus, that by beholding Him we may become changed into His image, from glory to glory. Have you discovered how much of a fight that can be? But we are invited *not* to fight when it comes to the fight of sin. And the struggle to allow God to do the fighting for us can be the greatest fight of all. In fact, it is called the greatest battle ever fought, this warfare against self and self-dependence and self-effort.

But for those who are willing to learn about the kingdom of heaven, for those who are willing to allow the Lord to fight for them, victory is assured. We can join the disciples in rejoicing in the good news that the servants of God do not have to fight, because the battle has already been won.

Chapter 9
You Can't Be Forgiven Unless You Forgive

I teach a class called the Dynamics of Christian Living. One day a student asked, "Would it be possible to flunk this class and still go to heaven?" Another student reversed the question and asked, "Would it be possible to get an A in this class and go the other place?"

I had opportunity to ponder those questions one day when word came about a student who had taken my class and had gotten an A. Later this student went to live with some of my parishioners, but he didn't seem to think it was necessary to pay his rent. Then, when my church members decided that it was time for the student to move to other accommodations, the student took several expensive items from the house and moved to another state.

When I heard the story, I was so upset about it that I asked the people what they were doing to bring the student to justice. They said, "Nothing. What can you do when someone has moved out of state?" And I thought, Maybe I could write to this student and tell him that unless he makes this right, I am changing his grade from an A to an F. Maybe that would help!

There's a story Jesus told about the kingdom that is similar to this episode. It is found in Matthew 18:23-35. "Therefore is the kingdom of heaven likened unto a certain king, which would take account of his servants. And when he had begun to reckon, one was brought unto him, which owed him ten thousand talents. But forasmuch as he had not to pay, his lord commanded him to be sold, and his wife, and children, and all that he had, and payment to be made. The servant therefore fell down, and worshipped him, saying, Lord, have patience with me, and I will pay thee all. Then the lord of that servant was moved with compassion, and loosed him, and forgave him the debt.

"But the same servant went out, and found one of his fellowservants, which owed him an hundred pence: and he laid hands on him, and took him by the throat, saying, Pay me that thou owest. And his fellowservant fell down at his feet, and besought him, saying, Have patience with me, and I will pay thee all. And he would not: but went and cast him into prison, till he should pay the debt.

"So when his fellowservants saw what was done, they were very sorry, and came and told unto their lord all that was done. Then his lord, after that he had called him, said unto him, O thou wicked servant, I forgave thee all that debt, because thou desiredst me: shouldest not thou also have had compassion on thy fellowservant, even as I had pity on thee? And his lord was wroth, and delivered him to the tormenters, till he should pay all that was due unto him. So likewise shall my heavenly Father do also unto you, if ye from your hearts forgive not every one his brother their trespasses."

Is the King Trustworthy?

Would you be willing to trust this king? Do you think he is a good king? You may say, It depends on who you are in the story. All right, who *are* you in the story?

If you are the one who went to the king and told on the unforgiving servant, then you're a man of action like the king. He took care of the problem right away.

If you are the man who owed the hundred pence, you like the king. You're glad to see your tormenter behind bars. You think the king is fair and just.

But if you are the one who owed the ten thousand talents and had thought you had escaped prison, you probably are not too happy with the king, isn't that right?

And then Jesus says, "This is the way My Father is going to

treat you." Sounds like a pretty severe God, complete with hell and brimstone, doesn't it? Would you like to be delivered to the tormenters by such a king?

This is a hard parable. The meaning is not on the surface. But as we attempt to grapple with it, let's back up two verses to what came just before. Peter and Jesus were talking. "Then came Peter to him, and said, Lord, how oft shall my brother sin against me and I forgive him? till seven times?"

Do you like Peter? He was always out in front, opening his mouth before he knew what he was going to say! He thought he had come up with a good idea here. The Pharisees limited forgiveness to three times—sort of a forgiveness ball game, three strikes and you're out. Peter had doubled their number, and then added one for good measure, making seven, the perfect number.

And he was all ready for Jesus to respond, "Why bless you, Peter, what a beautiful thought!"

Instead, Jesus suggested he multiply seven by 70! Obviously He was recommending unlimited forgiveness. Then He tells the story of a man who owes the equivalent of $20 million. He's forgiven, but refuses to forgive another man who owes him about $30. So the king throws him into prison, and Jesus says, "This is the way My Father is."

Seems incongruous, doesn't it? But let's examine it more closely and try to find the truth Jesus was presenting.

The drama of this story really comes in three parts. Let's look at each part separately.

Part I—The $20 Million Debt

This man owes $20 million, and it says he has not wherewith to pay. Well of course! How many of us, if we owed that kind of money, could pay? But the man doesn't realize his desperate condition. It says he falls down before the king crying, "Have patience with me, and I will pay thee all."

Now either he is a fool, or he is trying to con the king. He pretends to worship the king, but in reality, he's worshiping himself. He thinks that somehow he's big enough to pay his debt. And in this parable, which is really a parable about salvation, the man realizes neither the enormity of his debt nor his helplessness to pay it.

Are you in debt? Oh, we're not talking about the house payment and the car payment and the gas and electricity and tuition for the kids in school. The apostle Paul put it this way in Romans 1, "I am debtor." He was talking about the debt we owe to Jesus, the debt we can never repay.

When we come before the King, how foolish we would be to say, "Have patience with me, and I will pay." We can't pay. We're in debt to Jesus, and we don't have even one dime to put toward our account.

But the man in the parable is offered forgiveness for his debt. It says that the king forgave him. But there's something important that we need to begin noticing here. Forgiveness is a two-way street. If you are forgiven, you have to accept the forgiveness that has been offered. The offer of forgiveness is not enough.

There have been times in the history of our legal system when someone was awarded a pardon but refused to accept it. The first time it happened, it took some discussion and consideration before we knew how to handle it. What if someone doesn't accept the pardon? And the conclusion was reached that if a pardon is refused, then the person isn't pardoned after all. It's as simple as that!

How do we know the man did not accept the pardon? Because of his reaction! How would you react, if someone were to come to you today and say, "All of your debts are canceled as of right now. You don't owe anything anymore." Would you walk away without even saying thank you? The evidence in the story is that the man didn't even do that. He just walked away.

Part II—The $30 Debt

The first thing the $20 million debtor did, instead of falling at the feet of the king in gratitude and love, was to go out and nail one of his fellowservants, who owed him a paltry $30. He threatened him, and even when his fellowservant offered the same plea he had just made before the king, his heart was not softened. He had him cast into prison.

Why did he do this? Maybe he was simply greedy, and although he was glad to have the weight of the $20 million off his back, he thought this would be a good chance to get some pocket money to celebrate with! But there's another possibility. If he has in reality not accepted the king's offer of pardon, then perhaps he was intending to recoup his resources and pay the king what he owed. Maybe he didn't like charity. Maybe he was determined not to be indebted to the king. Maybe he didn't want to live with the sense of obligation that the forgiveness might give him.

This man had a long, hard winter ahead if he was going to return the $20 million, $30 at a time! The ratio of the debts was a million and a half to one. So he had a lot of hard labor ahead of him. But whatever his motive, one fact is clear. He did not treat his fellowservant as he had been treated by the king.

Part III—He's in the Jail House Now!

There seems to be a code in most schools, and perhaps in most of the world as well, that it is not too cool to snitch on someone else. Young people have a particularly strong code of ethics that you don't tell, you don't squeal, you don't fink, or whatever the current term for it is. They have all kinds of labels for it. But none of them are complimentary! It is considered an almost unforgivable sin to tattle.

But either the code of ethics in the court of this king was different, or perhaps there are some things that are so blatant, so bad, that you can't help but go and tell. So some of the servants told the king what has happened, and the king was wroth.

The king called the first man back into his presence. He sentenced him to prison and delivered him to the tormenters until he should pay his debt.

There are those today who don't want a God who gets angry. But this king was wroth. They don't want a God who is active in judgment. But this king sent his servant to prison, to the tormenters. He didn't just allow him to experience the results of his wrongdoing. He moved in and brought the results to bear.

And it says he was to stay in the prison until he had paid all his debt. That was going to take awhile, wasn't it? What a strange story!

Contrast Between the Two Kingdoms

One thing we can learn from this story is that there are two kingdoms, the kingdom of heaven and the kingdom of this world. And their method of operation is strikingly different. In the kingdom of this world, you get what you earn, and you earn what you get. You work your way. We don't know a whole lot about forgiveness and gifts and mercy in this kingdom in which we live.

People have struggled with this difference. And when they understand that the kingdom of heaven is on the gift system and that merit and earning and wages and credit are not a part of that kingdom, they find it hard to grasp.

But in the kingdom of heaven, we are freely forgiven, and, in turn we are to freely forgive. There is no forgiveness available for the one who is unforgiving toward others. But that brings us to a problem. Is it our willingness to forgive that causes God to forgive us? The Lord's prayer says, "Forgive us our debts *as* we forgive our debtors." It doesn't say, Forgive us *because* we forgive." Can there be a difference?

Does that help your understanding of this story? Or do you have trouble understanding the difference between *because* and *as?*

Let's look at two possible solutions. You may decide for yourself which category you think this man belongs in, but there seems to be two possibilities to account for someone who has been forgiven to now be unforgiving.

The first, as we have already mentioned, is to never accept forgiveness in the first place. Forgiveness always requires two parties. If there has been a break in our relationship, either between us and someone else, or between us and God, both must become willing for reconciliation to take place. Otherwise there will be no reconciliation.

Have you ever, in your human relationships, found yourself estranged from someone you loved? Have you offered forgiveness and had it refused? When that happens, even if you were in the right, the relationship dies unless the offer of forgiveness is accepted.

When Jesus died on the cross, He made it possible for forgiveness to be offered to everybody—regardless of who you are or what you have done or where you come from. Because of Jesus, you can be forgiven. It doesn't matter whether you owe $20 million or only $30. Forgiveness is offered freely to every person.

But as beautiful as that is, it isn't worth a dime for me unless I am willing to accept it. So if I have not accepted the forgiveness the King has extended, then the time of judgment and the going to prison is inevitable.

I don't believe this man ever accepted the forgiveness of the king. There was no evidence of appreciation, there is evidence he was still intent on repayment, and there is evidence he didn't know what forgiveness was all about by the way he treated his fellowservant.

Is it possible to accept of God's forgiveness and then turn around and be unforgiving to another? Of course it is. And if that is possible, then what is the solution? Are we supposed to try hard to forgive others, so that God can forgive us?

Examining this parable from another aspect, it indicates that it is possible for one to be truly forgiven, and yet end up not forgiving his brother. And here's how that can happen. A person may have *once* received forgiveness, but subsequently his unmerciful spirit shows that he now rejects God's pardoning love. He has now separated himself from God and is in the same condition as before he was forgiven. If all that was needed was to once accept God's forgiveness and then automatically, forever after, you would be a forgiving person, there would be no need for the warning inherent in this story, as well as in the Lord's prayer.

We might call this the "so long as" principle. So long as we are connected to God and depending on Him, sin has no power over us. It makes no difference what sin you are talking about. As soon as we separate from God and His control, we are in the same condition as before. The religion of Christ is based on relationship, never behavior. When we come to Christ in the first place, He forgives our sins. And all of our bad behavior is forgotten. But if we choose to separate from Christ, all of our good behavior is of no value! Ezekiel 3:20 talks about that.

The simple truth is that if we are connected to Christ and under His control, we *will be* forgiving towards others. And if we break from that dependence, we *will not be* forgiving. The unforgiving spirit is not the cause; it is the result of having separated from God.

This is inherent in the passage. Notice, it is not enough to *act* as if you are forgiving. What does it say? It says, This is what my Father will do to you, "if ye *from your hearts* forgive not every one his brother." Matthew 18:35. Emphasis supplied.

The only way we can forgive from the heart is if we have had our hearts broken and subdued by the Spirit of God. It's not something we can work on ourselves. It's not something we offer to God—rather it is something He offers to us. And it is ours *so long as* we accept it.

But the King Was Wroth

Are you still nervous about the angry King? Just remember—it doesn't say at whom he was wroth. It just says he was wroth—presumably at His unforgiving servant. But there is another way to look at the King's wrath. God has always been wroth at sin. He hates it, doesn't He? He is always wroth at the deception in His universe that would lead His own creation to separate from Him and die. Don't you want God to be angry at that?

But you can still see a God who chokes with tears as He considers one who has walked away from Him. He is eternally committed to allowing us to choose freely. But the pain that comes to His great heart of love, when we choose against Him, we will never be able to understand. God's heart is broken anew each time He offers reconciliation and pardon, and one of His children refuses to accept His forgiveness.

We cannot pay the debt we owe to Him. We cannot pay one penny of it. All we can do is to go to His feet and say, "Jesus paid it all. All to Him I owe." And the debt of love that we owe is as big as all eternity.

Chapter 10
The Least of These My Brethren

"When the Son of man shall come in his glory, and all the holy angels with him, then shall he sit upon the throne of his glory: and before him shall be gathered all nations: and he shall separate them one from another, as a shepherd divideth his sheep from the goats." Matthew 25:31, 32.

One of the teachings about the kingdom of heaven that Jesus repeated over and over again was the fact of judgment. He talked about an investigative judgment in Matthew 22, when the king comes in to examine his guests, to see who has on the wedding garment. He talks about the net that is cast into the sea and gathers fish of every kind in Matthew 13. And then when it is drawn to shore, the fishermen sit down and separate between the good and the bad, keeping the good and casting the bad away.

In this description of the time of judgment in Matthew 25, we are given a clue as to what determines the outcome in that day of decision.

Let's continue reading the description in verses 33 through 40. "He shall set the sheep on his right hand, but the goats on the left. Then shall the King say unto them on his right hand, Come, ye blessed of my Father, inherit the kingdom prepared for you from the foundation of the world: for I was an hungred, and ye gave me meat: I was thirsty, and ye gave me drink: I was a stranger, and ye took me in: naked, and ye clothed me: I was sick, and ye visited me: I was in prison, and ye came unto me."

And when the righteous express surprise that they have done any of these things, He continues, "Inasmuch as ye have done it unto one of the least of these my brethren, ye have done it unto me."

So the decision in the judgment is represented as turning upon this one point: What have we done for Christ by ministering to others? It could almost sound like a legalistic approach. Maybe we don't earn our salvation by good works in terms of overcoming sin—but are we to conclude that we earn our salvation by good works in terms of humanitarianism? In that case, would it not be well for us to join in with the social gospel?

Have you ever looked at your own life and compared it with this list of good deeds, which Christ commends? Have you ever tried to count how many hitchhikers you have picked up and whether or not you opened your guest room the last time some traveling singing group came to town? How many cans did you donate to the food drive at Thanksgivingtime, and have you been faithful in giving your clothes to the Good Will, instead of throwing them in the garbage? How about the hospital visits and prison ministry? Hours of Christian help work? Maybe pieces of missionary literature distributed? How does it all fit into the picture?

The Parable of the Talents

Let's leave the judgment scene for a few minutes and spend some time with another of Jesus' parables of the kingdom—the parable of the talents. You may recall, a man was traveling to a far country (Matthew 25:14), and he called together his servants and delivered unto them his goods. He gave one five talents, another two talents, and yet another only one talent. And he went his way.

The servants that had been given five talents and two talents went to work and doubled their Master's investment. But the man who had received only one talent buried his talent in a field.

When the lord of the servants returned, he was pleased with the increase from the two servants, but dealt severely with the one-talent servant, because of his actions. His one talent was taken away and given to the man who had ten talents, and it says, "Unto every one that hath shall be given, and he shall have abundance: but from him that hath not shall be taken away even that which he hath. And cast ye the unprofitable servant into outer darkness: there shall be weeping and gnashing of teeth." Verses 29, 30.

Again, judgment language, describing the time when the results are evaluated and justice is meted out.

This parable reminds us of the absolute necessity of service in the Christian life. It is not enough to receive—we must also give. If we do not grow, we die. It's as simple as that. And it is as we work with Christ in working for others that we are working out our own salvation.

We are not to wait to begin our work for Christ. We are to follow through on the initial desire to share, for no sooner does one come to Christ than there is born in his heart a desire to make known to others what a precious Friend he has found in Jesus. The saving and sanctifying truth cannot be shut up in his heart. If we are clothed with the righteousness of Christ and are filled with the joy of His indwelling Spirit, we shall not be able to hold our peace. If we have tasted and seen that the Lord is good, we shall have something to tell. Like Philip when he found the Saviour, we shall invite others into His presence.

So, no sooner does one come to Christ than he is given a talent or two or five. He is given the equipment to get started. He sees the love of Christ, and he has something to tell. In fact, the saving and sanctifying truth cannot be shut up in his heart. He will not be able to hold his peace.

Then how was it possible for this man with the one talent to bury it in the earth? He should have been constrained to take it out and double it. Isn't it supposed to happen automatically? If the impulse or desire to witness comes spontaneously when we have been born again, then at first glance it would seem that this warning about burying talents would be completely unnecessary.

But look again. Is the parable saying that it is impossible to *try* to hide the truth and bury it out of sight? Or is it only saying that it is impossible to succeed? The man in the parable thought he could keep the one talent to himself, but he found out that a talent is not something you can keep. You either use it, or you lose it.

You Can't Keep Your Parakeet in Tupperware!

Suppose I told you that you cannot keep your parakeet shut up in a Tupperware container, that if you have a parakeet, you will not be able to keep him in your lettuce crisper. Would that mean that your parakeet was so strong that no matter how hard you tried, he would not be able to break out and get away? Or would that mean that if you were foolish enough to try it, you wouldn't have a parakeet very long—all you'd have would be a pathetic little pile of feathers?

That's the way it is in the Christian witness. We shall not be able to hold our peace, because if we try, we lose it! We cannot shut the truth up in our hearts, because we lose it if it is not shared. And if we don't tell what the Lord has done for us while we have something to tell, it won't be long before we will no longer have anything to say. There is danger for those who do little or nothing for Christ. The grace of God will not long abide in the soul of him who, having had great privileges and opportunities, remains silent. Such a person will soon find that he has nothing to tell.

The basic premise of the Christian religion is that all are workers. We may work in different ways, our talents may differ, but there is one common denominator. We will have something to tell about Jesus.

Sometimes people talk about the silent witness. My, but the silent witness is popular! Everybody wants to be a silent witness. I've heard church members say, "If I just bake a nice loaf of bread and take it to my sick neighbor, I'm witnessing. If I keep my car washed and my yard neat, I'm witnessing. If I work hard at my job and am honest in my business dealing, I'm witnessing."

Are those things important? Sure they are. But would it be

possible for an atheist to bake a loaf of good bread and take it to a sick neighbor? Would it be possible for an infidel to keep his car washed and his lawn mowed? Would it be possible for the agnostic to work hard at his job and deal honestly in his business?

The difference between the Christian and the one who accepts only a social gospel is that the Christian has something to *tell*. And if he doesn't tell, he soon will find that he no longer has anything to tell!

What have you had to tell about the Lord Jesus this week? Have you been able to go beyond being a nice person, a good neighbor, a moralist? Have you tasted and seen that the Lord is good? That's the starting place. You have to begin in your closet, getting acquainted with Him for yourself. But you don't stay in the closet. You go about your day, but with a difference: you have something to tell. You have a message that the one who does not know God does not have. And that is what makes the difference.

Back to the Judgment

With that in mind, let's go back to the judgment scene. Is Christ telling His disciples that the decision in the judgment will be based on how many sick calls and food baskets and alms for the poor have been given? No! All of those things are good in themselves, but there is far more involved. Christ Himself told us not to labor for the meat which perishes, but for everlasting life. How could He be settling the decisions for eternal life on the basis of food baskets and articles of clothing given away, valuable though those may be?

Let's look a little deeper and see the spiritual meaning of this parable about the judgment. He says that in ministering to others, we are ministering to Him. And He says, "I was hungry, and ye gave me meat." Is that talking about physical food, or could it also be talking about the Bread of Life? Isn't He the One who said, in John 6, "My flesh is meat indeed, and my blood is drink indeed"? "This is the bread which cometh down from heaven, that a man may eat thereof, and not die." Verses

55, 50. So, what have you done to share the bread of life? That's the question.

Jesus said, "I was thirsty, and ye gave me drink." Was Jesus talking about the waters of this world? He's the One who said it in John 4:13, 14, "Whosoever drinketh of this water shall thirst again: but whosoever drinketh of the water that I shall give him shall never thirst; but the water that I shall give him shall be in him a well of water springing up into everlastingl life."

"I was a stranger and ye took me in." When we bring someone to Christ, then it can be said, "Now therefore ye are no more strangers and foreigners, but fellowcitizens with the saints, and of the household of God." Ephesians 2:19.

"Naked and ye clothed me." When we ourselves have been clothed in the garments of Christ's righteousness, we can offer the same to others, sharing with them the "white raiment, that thou mayest be clothed, and that the shame of thy nakedness do not appear." Revelation 3:18.

"I was sick, and ye visited me." Those who have never learned of Christ and the good news of the salvation provided are sick. In fact, we are told, "The whole head is sick, and the whole heart faint. From the sole of the foot even unto the head there is no soundness in it; but wounds, and bruises, and putrifying sores." Isaiah 1:5, 6.

"I was in prison, and ye came unto me." Those who are captives to Satan's control are in his prison house. The time will come when all will look upon him, and say, "Is this the man . . . that opened not the house of his prisoners?" Isaiah 14:16, 17. The worst kind of bondage there is is a slavery to sin, and the greatest freedom comes in the salvation Christ has to offer. There are people today who are behind bars, but who are free. But there are far more who are free, yet who are prisoners.

In the time of judgment, when the records of all are brought to light, what will the question be? It will be whether or not we have continued in fellowship and communion with Christ and in service with Him. We cannot long continue to fellowship with Him unless we join Him in working for a world that is in need. In ministering to others, we find not only our own salvation, but the greatest happiness of our lives as well.

Chapter 11
A Fool and His Money

"A fool and his money are soon parted," or so the old saying goes. It seemed to hold true for the foolish prodigal, who wasted his substance in a far country, as we noticed earlier. But Jesus told another parable about another fool, and the basis of his foolishness was hoarding his money, not squandering it!

The story is found in Luke 12:16-21. "He spake a parable unto them, saying, The ground of a certain rich man brought forth plentifully: and he thought within himself, saying, What shall I do, because I have no room where to bestow my fruits? And he said, This will I do: I will pull down my barns, and build greater; and there will I bestow all my fruits and my goods. And I will say to my soul, Soul, thou hast much goods laid up for many years; take thine ease, eat, drink, and be merry. But God said unto him, Thou fool, this night thy soul shall be required of thee: then whose shall those things be, which thou hast provided? So is he that layeth up treasure for himself, and is not rich toward God."

It must be easy to be foolish if you are rich. Jesus told one of His mini-parables in Matthew 19: "Verily I say unto you, That a rich man shall hardly enter into the kingdom of heaven. And again I say unto you, It is easier for a camel to go through the eye of a needle, than for a rich man to enter into the kingdom of God." Verses 23, 24.

So it doesn't look too hopeful for the rich person, does it? Are you rich? Your answer to that question would probably be based on whom you are being compared to. Are you rich compared to John D. Rockefeller? Are you rich compared to an orphan on the streets of Bombay, India?

And how do you figure your riches? Sometimes the ones who live in the fancy houses and drive expensive cars simply have a higher line of credit than the rest of us, and maybe even less money in the pocket. When you count your assets, do you consider your money in the bank exclusively? Or your possessions? Or your potential earning power? Those in the financial world consider at least those three.

If you want to add the things that are worth more than money, such as health and happiness and love of family and friends, then you may find yourself very wealthy.

But this parable about the rich fool gives at least three warnings to the rich—and in one way or another, they can apply to every one of us.

A Coin out of Circulation Is No Good

There is no value to money that is not in use. The woman in the parable of the lost coin searched diligently for the coin that was out of circulation. If she had never found it, if it had remained buried in the dust and debris, it wouldn't have been of value to her, or to anybody else.

So the first mistake this rich fool made was to try to hoard his riches. He didn't invest them. He didn't share them. He didn't give them away. He wasn't able to use them all for himself right away. And so he hoarded them.

Some of us may have to decide how much to put aside for a rainy day, how much to keep in reserve for future emergencies. Others of us may spend it as fast as we get it and never have a problem with hoarding our money. But this parable is talking about something more than just dollars and cents.

As we noticed in the last chapter, it is foolish to try to hoard the grace of God. It was meant to be shared. When we receive a rich blessing from the Lord, the last thing in the world we should try to do is hang onto it. It was given to give away. Jesus said, "Freely ye have received, freely give." Matthew 10:8. And in the giving away, we find our hearts prepared to receive even richer gifts from heaven.

The second mistake the rich fool made was to lay up treasure _for himself_. He was out for number one. It isn't a sin to be rich. Abraham was very rich (see Genesis 13:2); so was Job (see Job 1). In fact, the Bible says it is God who gives the power to get wealth. See Deuteronomy 8:18. This rich fool in the parable didn't need to get rid of every dime he had and live in poverty in order to live for others. But he could have shared the extra portion, instead of building the bigger and better barns, and then his treasure would have enriched others as well.

Again, it's not just money that can be used for self. Whatever talents or education or influence or riches that we possess, they are of value only as they are used to minister to others. When we use any of our treasure for ourselves, we miss the point of the gospel of the kingdom.

And third, this rich fool was not rich toward God. His very attitude gives it away when he said, Now it's time to eat, drink, and be merry. He wasn't interested in the things of the kingdom; he wasn't seeking to store up treasure in heaven. He was perfectly satisfied to keep his treasure right here on this earth.

And as in the old adage, this fool and his money were soon parted. That very night he and his money were parted. He had stored his treasure on earth, and when his time on this earth was done, his treasure was lost to him forever.

There must have been poor people in this rich man's country, in his neighborhood. Perhaps they cried to God for relief—and God had answered their prayers by sending extra to this rich man. But the rich man didn't do his part. God was sending to each the blessing most needed. For the rich man, the greatest blessing he could have received would have been to become involved in sharing his abundance with others.

No matter what your yearly income, no matter what your assets or your bank account, in one way or another, you are rich. It's the way in which you use your riches that is the crucial factor. Are you willing for God to work through you to answer the prayers of those who need the help you can give? Are you willing to put your treasure in heaven, where neither moth nor rust doth corrupt, and where thieves do not break through and steal? Are you not only rich in this world, but rich toward God? Are you willing to give to others as you continue to receive?

The wise man said it, "There is that scattereth, and yet increaseth; and there is that withholdeth more than is meet, but it tendeth to poverty." Proverbs 11:24.

The angels find their joy in giving. All of nature is constantly giving. The kingdom of heaven is based on giving and giving and giving again. The greatest gift of heaven, in giving Jesus for sinful man, has made it possible for us to be freed from the foolishness of serving self. Won't you accept again today the gift of the kingdom of heaven and, in turn, share that gift with those in your world? In no better way can you show your gratitude for His unspeakable Gift.